Kid's Box

New Generation

Caroline Nixon &
Michael Tomlinson

Starter

S

Class Book
with Digital Pack
American English

CAMBRIDGE

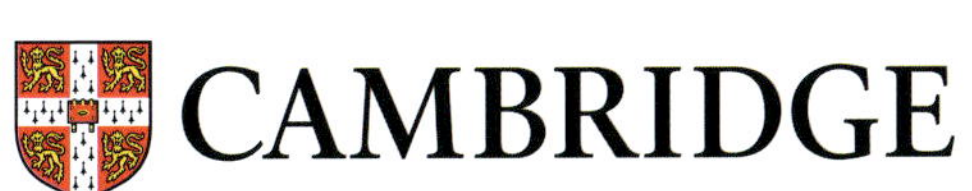

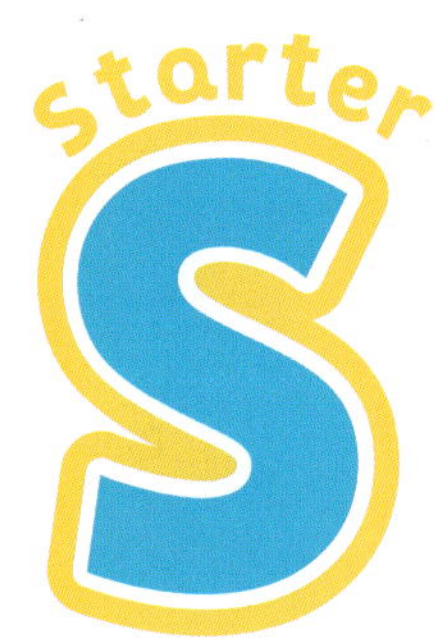

Language summary

1 Hi!

1 🎧 2–3 **Listen and point. Listen and repeat.**

2 🎵🎧 4 **Say the chant. Do the actions.**

Vocabulary presentation: names and numbers 1–3

1 🎧 5 **Listen and check (✓).**

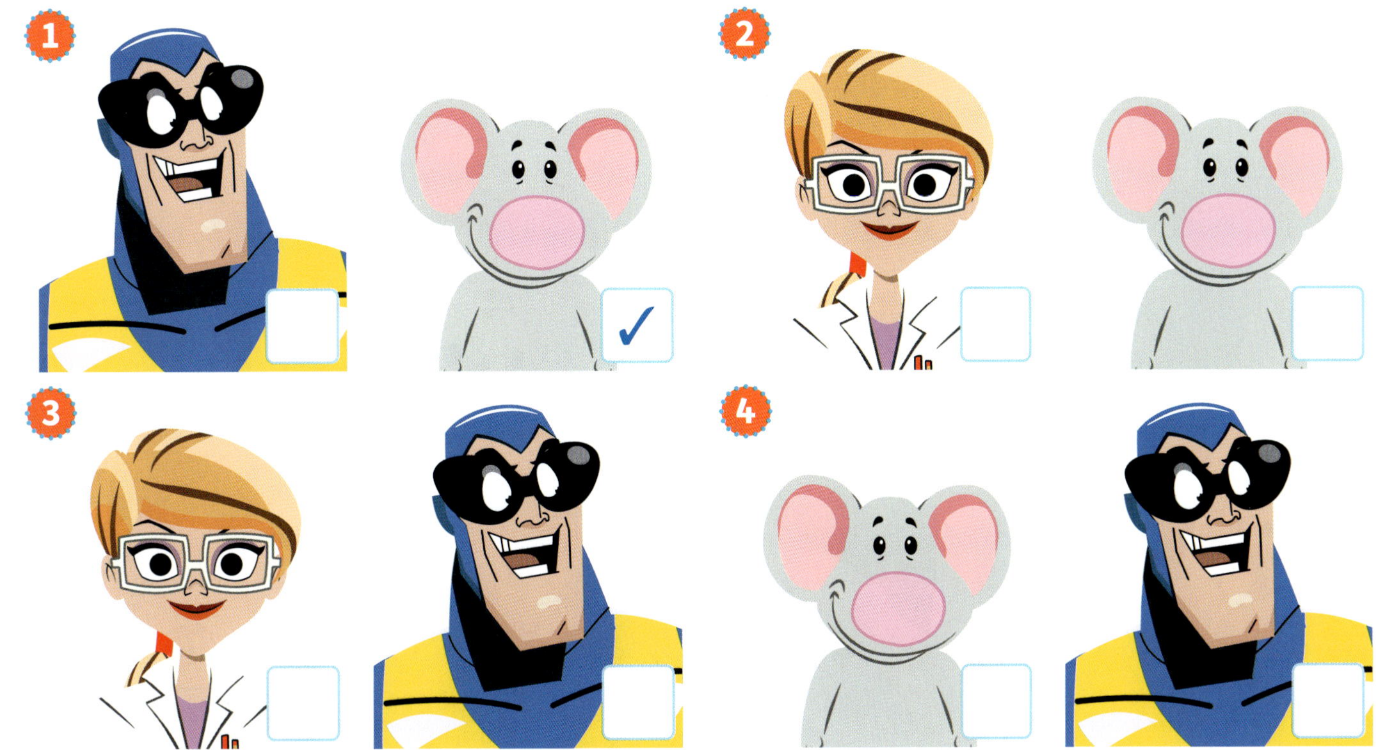

2 **Look and draw. Say the number.**

1

3	1	2
3	3	1
2	1	3

2

1	3	2
3	2	2
3	1	2

3

2	3	1
3	1	2
1	1	3

4

2	1	1
1	3	2
3	3	3

1 6-7 **Listen and point. Sing the song.**

2 **Ask and answer.**

Vocabulary presentation: numbers 1–6

 Look and draw. Say the numbers.

2	••

6	

3	

5	

1	

4	

2 🎧 8 ▶ Listen and circle.

1 🎧 9 ▶ Watch the video. Listen and act out the story.

Story: unit language in context

 🎧 10 Listen and circle. Who says it?

 Play and draw.

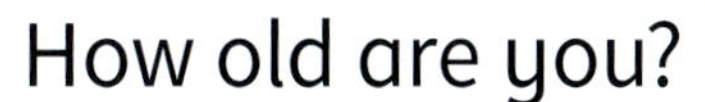

1 🎧 11 ▶ **Watch and say.**

2 **Ask, answer, and point.**

Sounds: _May, mouse, Matt, Monty, Maskman, Marie_

1 🎧 12 **Listen and stick.**

2 🎧 13 **Talk to Maskman.**

2 My class

1 🎧 14–15 **Listen and point. Listen and repeat.**

2 🎵🎧 16 **Say the chant. Do the actions.**

Vocabulary presentation: classroom objects

1 🎧 17 Listen and circle the number.

1   4   (5)

2   2   3

3   3   4

4   2   3

5   5   6

6   1   2

2 Look and complete.

Language presentation: classroom language

1 Listen and check (✓).

20

1

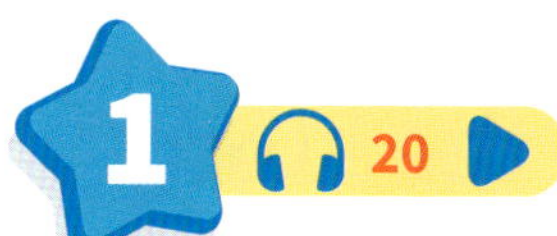

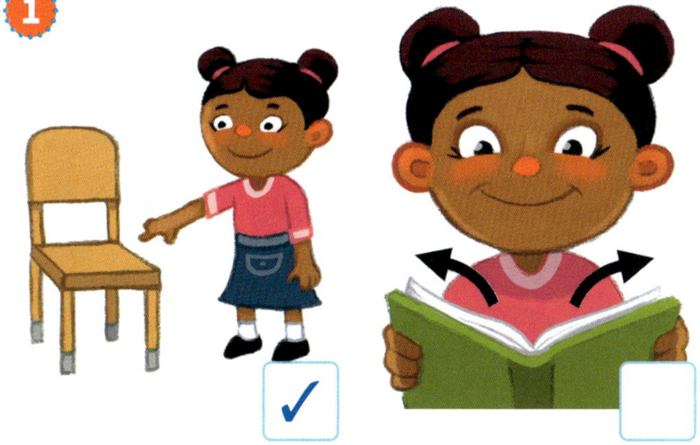

2

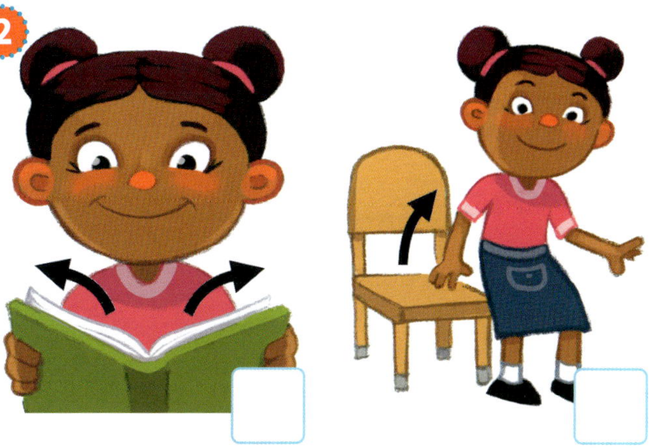

3

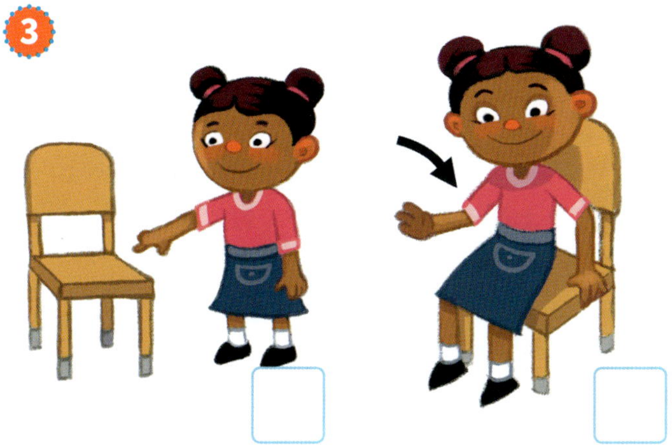

4

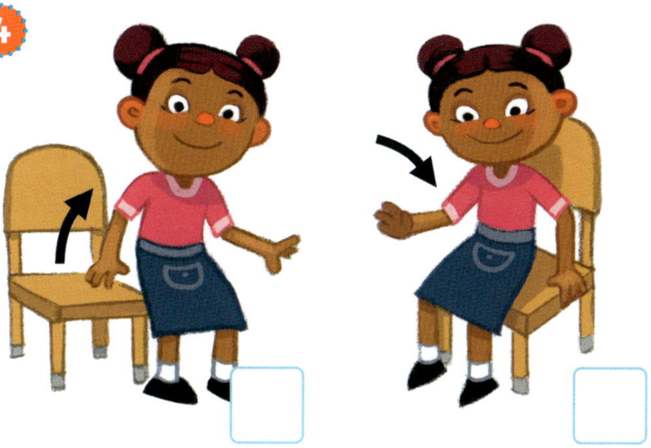

2 Draw your classroom. Say.

Me!

Watch the video. Listen and act out the story.

Story: unit language in context

 🎧 22 Listen and write the number.

1

2 Circle. Say and circle.

> Three tables.

> Yes, three tables.

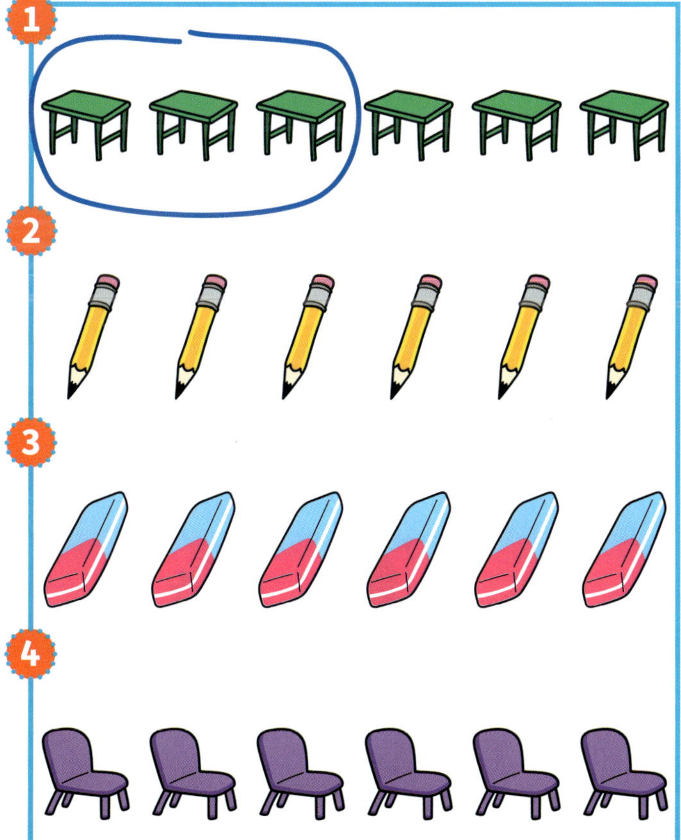

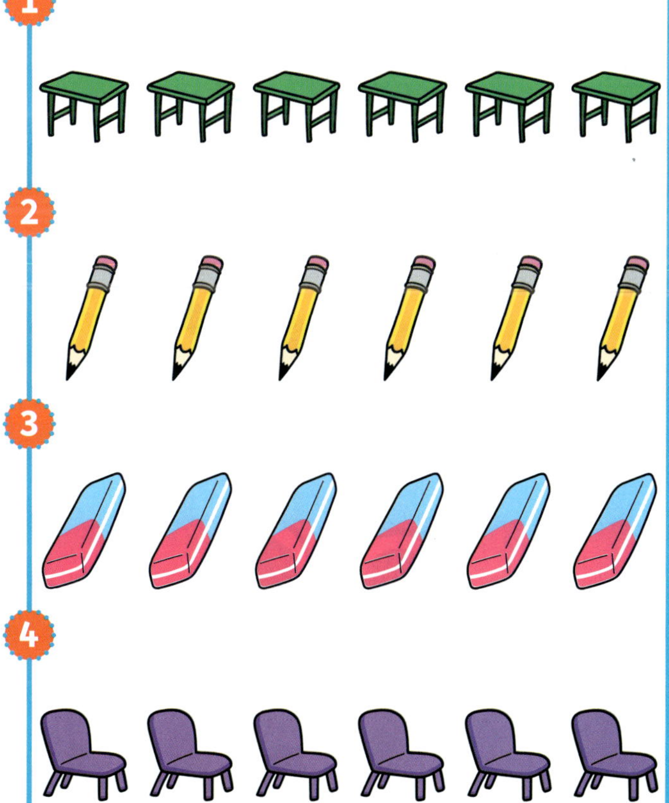

Monty's sounds

Watch and say.

2 **Ask and answer.**

   Sounds: _c_at, bl_a_ck, b_a_g

 **1** 🎧 24 **Listen and stick.**

2 🎧 25 **Talk to Maskman.**

Marie's math

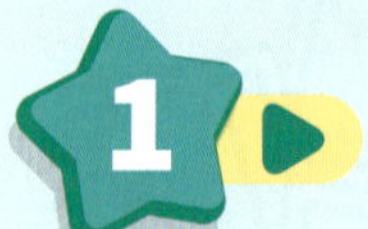

What shapes can I see?

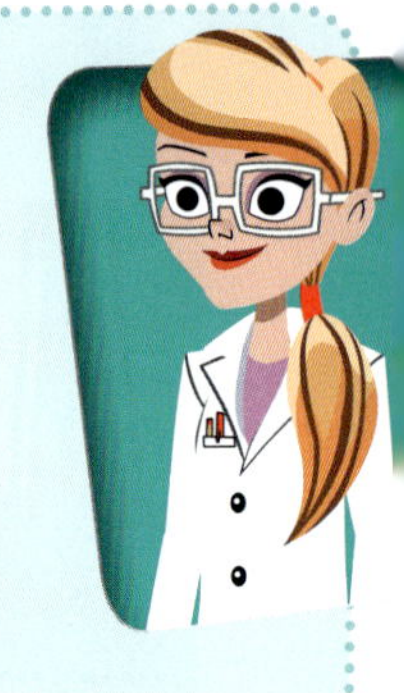

1 ▶ **Watch the video. Answer.**

2 🎧 26 **Listen and point. Say the shapes.**

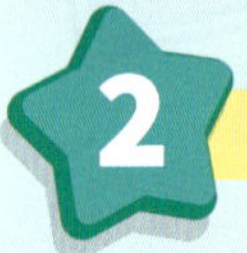

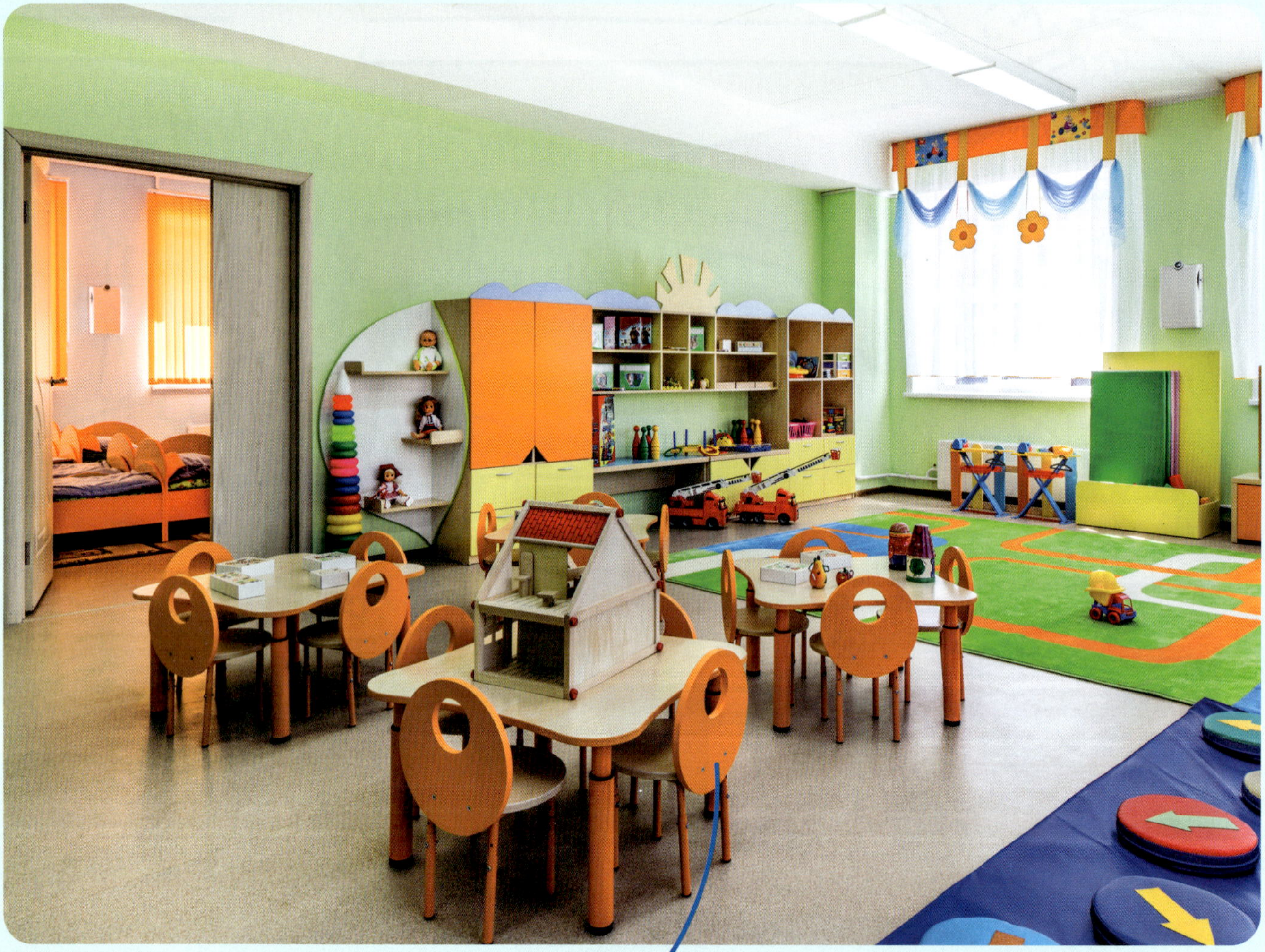

3 **Look and draw lines.**

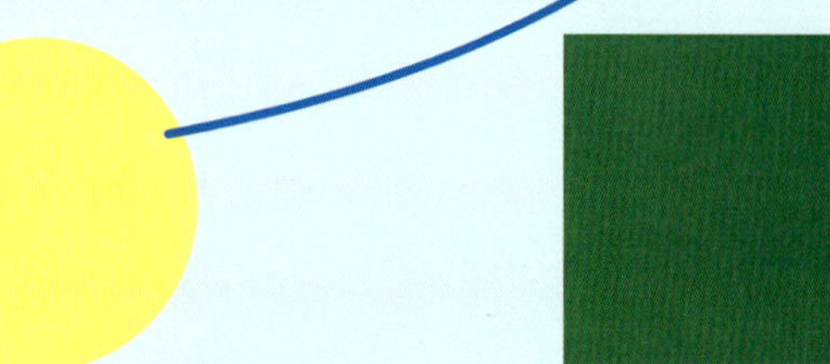

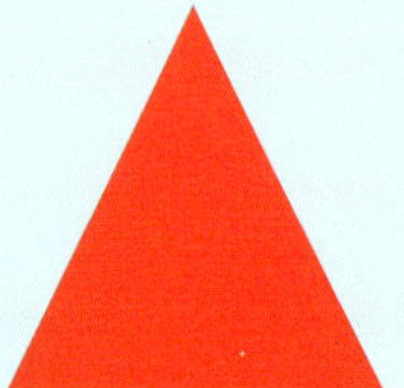

4 🎧 27 Listen and look. Count and write.

5 Look and draw. Color.

Project

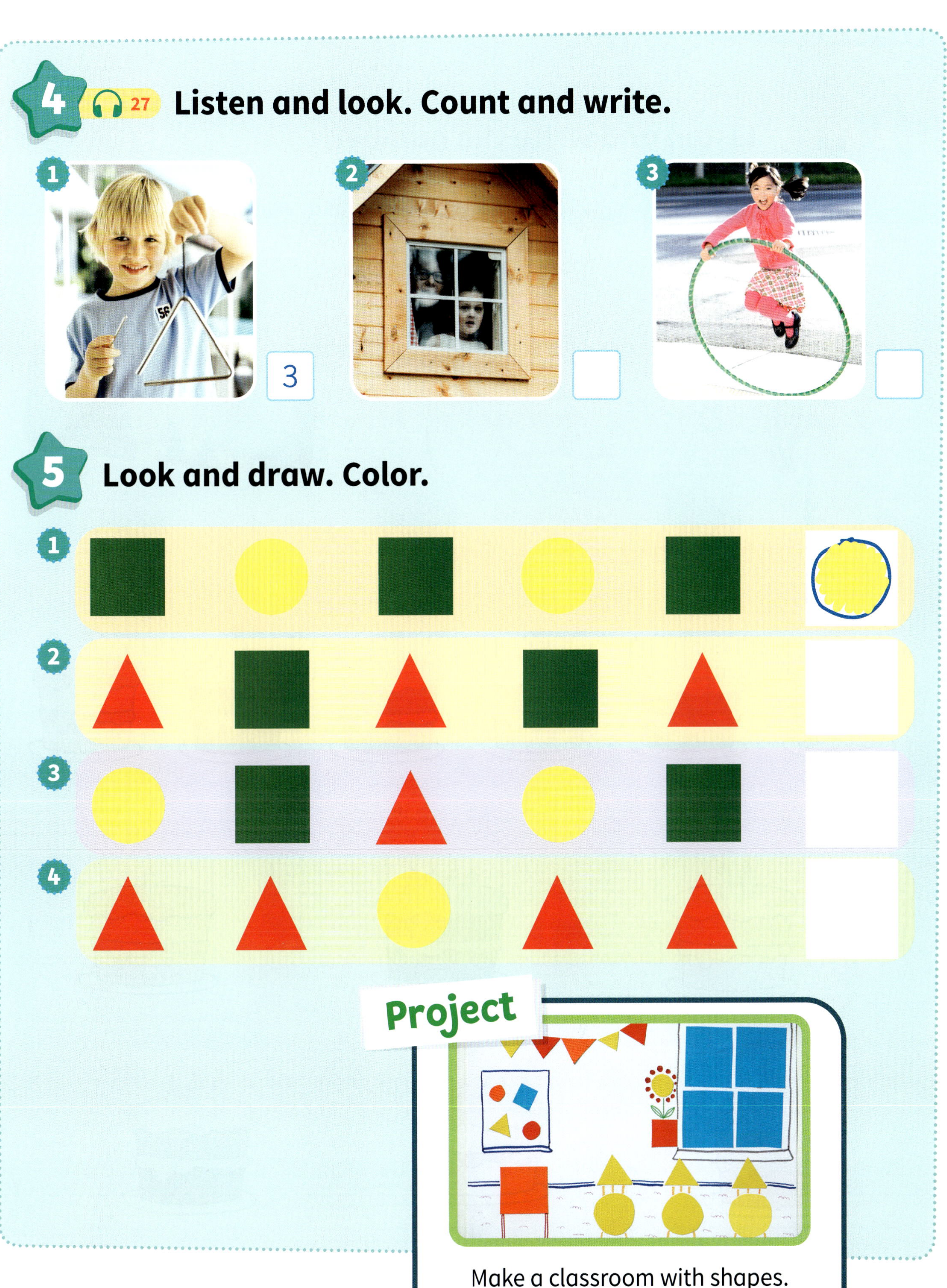

Make a classroom with shapes.

Maskman's practice

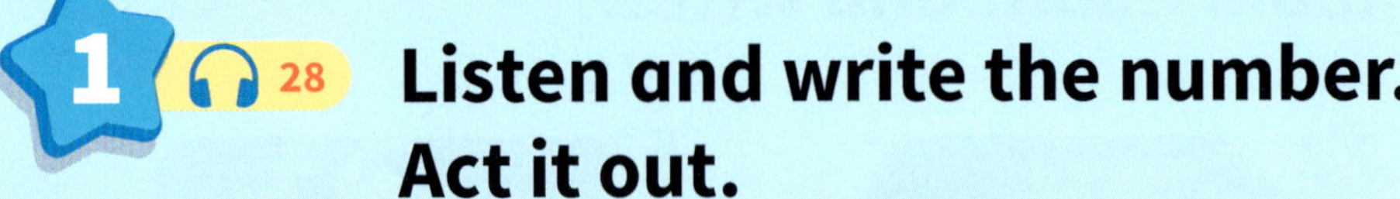

1 🎧 28 **Listen and write the number. Act it out.**

2  **Count and draw lines. Say.**

3 🎧 29 Look and count. Listen and circle.

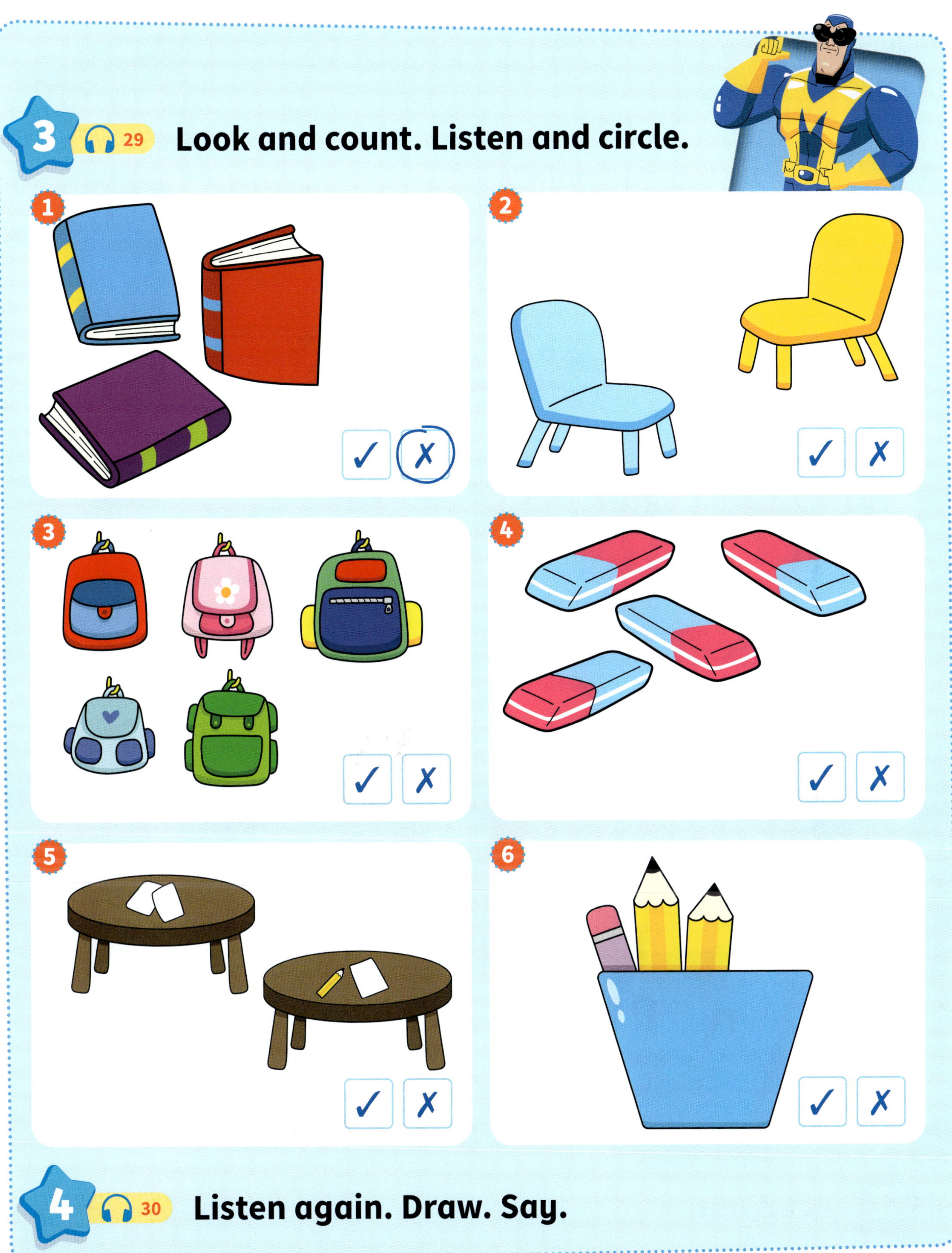

4 🎧 30 Listen again. Draw. Say.

Trevor's values

Asking nicely

1 🎧 31 **Listen and point.**

2 **Act it out.**

 Asking nicely: *Pass me the pencil, please. Here you are. Thank you.* | 🛡 social responsibilities

Review Units 1 and 2

1 🎧 32 Listen and circle the number.

1  
（5） 6

2 
2   3

3 
3   4

4 
1   2

2 🎧 33 Listen, count, and color.

1 

2 

3 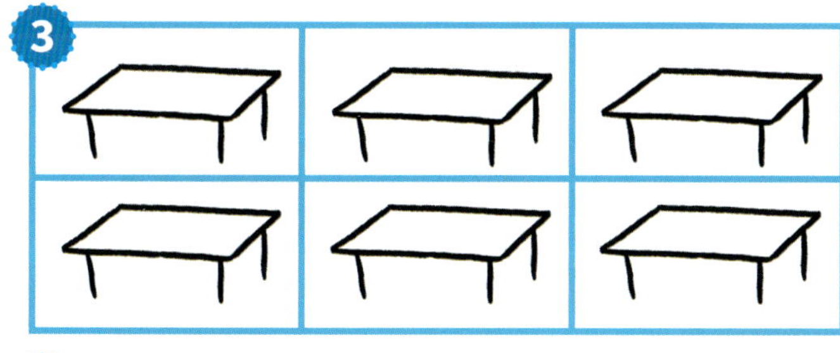

4 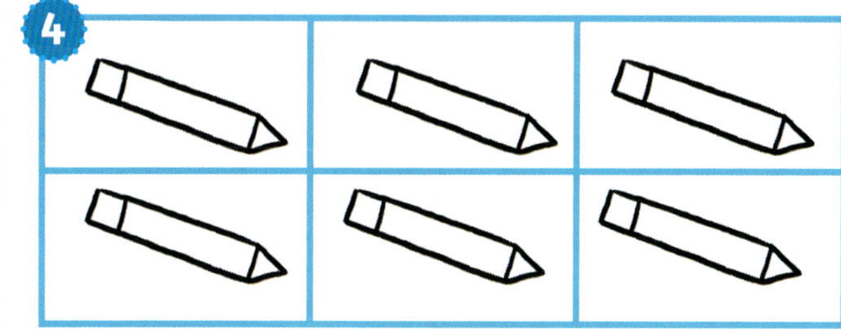

5 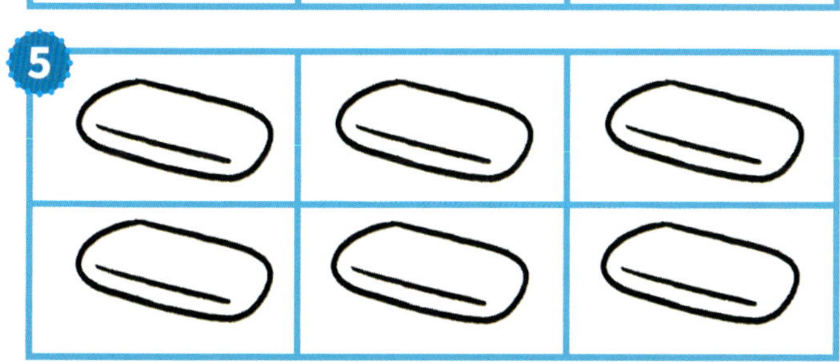

6 

3 My colors

Vocabulary presentation: colors

1 37 Listen and draw lines.

1 2 3

2 38 Listen and color.

1 2 3 4 5 6

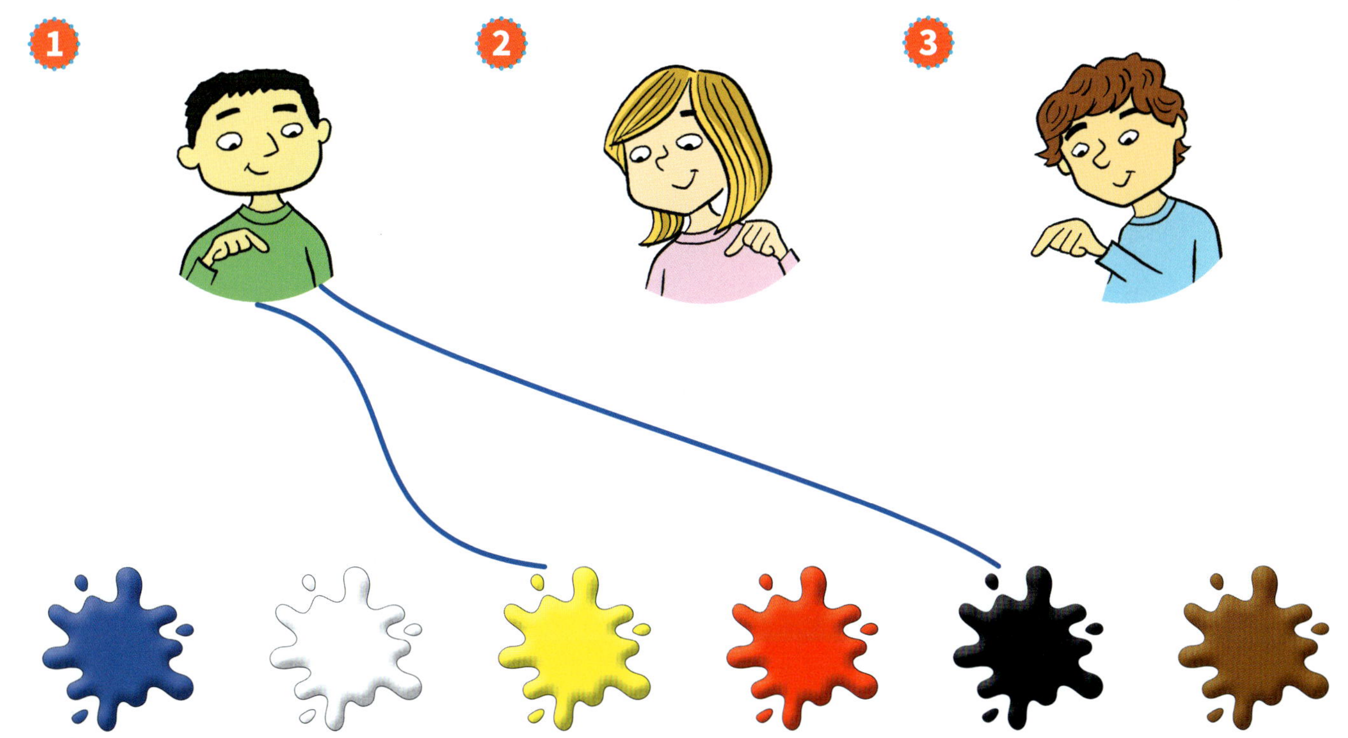

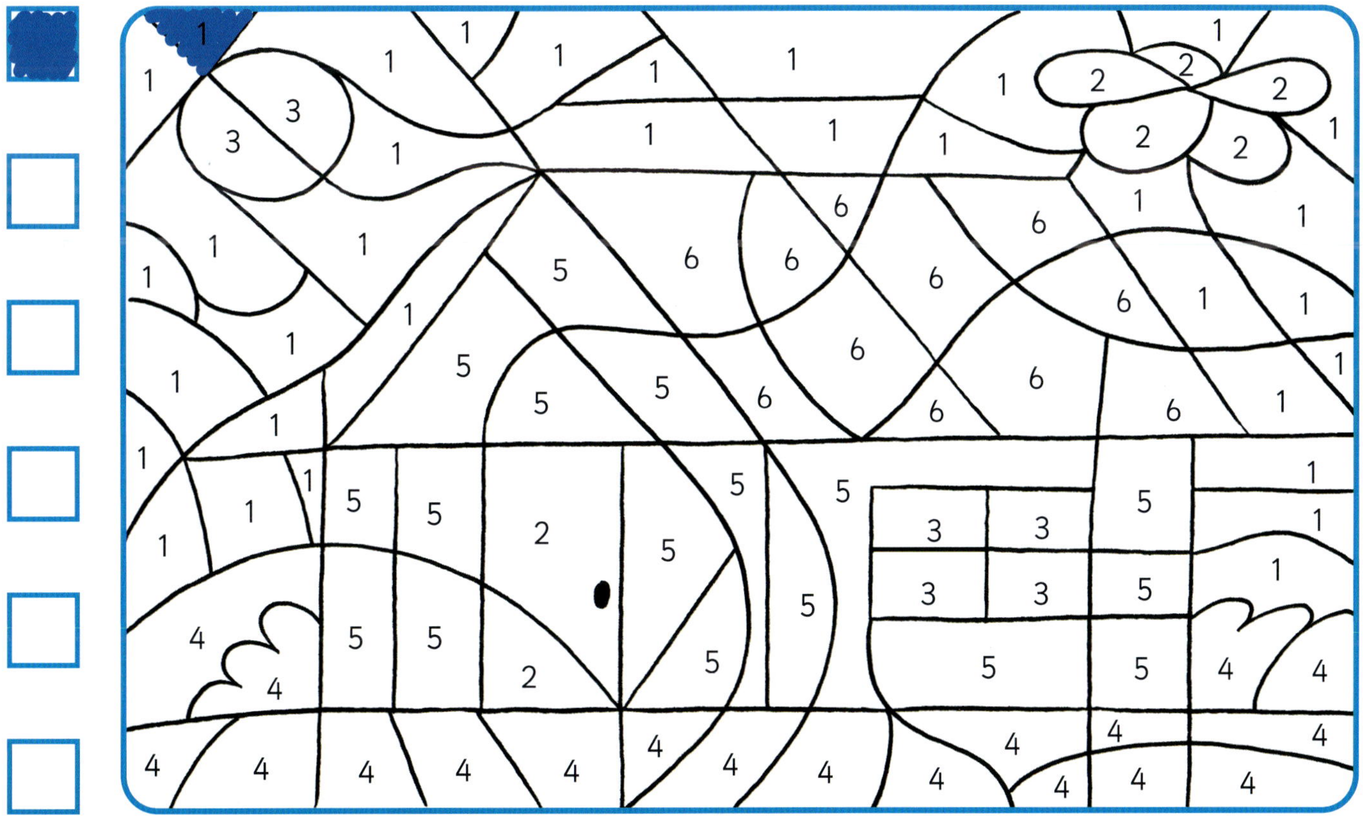

2 **Point and say.**

Language presentation: *It's a red pencil.*

1 🎧 41 Listen and color.

1 **2** **3**

4 **5** **6**

2 🎧 42 ▶ Listen, count, and answer.

1 🎧 43 ▶ **Watch the video. Listen and act out the story.**

1 44 Listen and color.

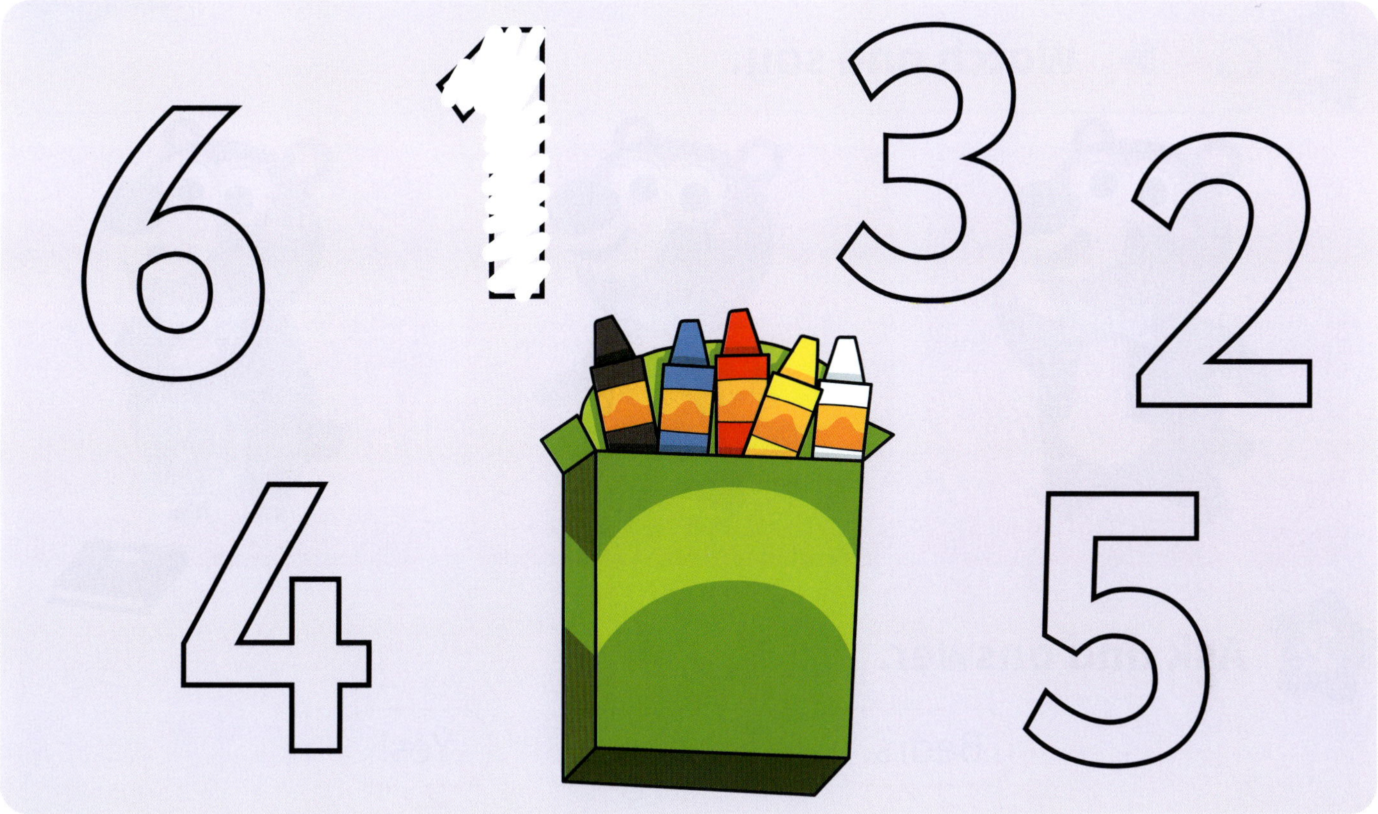

2 Color. Say and color.

Color number 1 black, please.

Yes, number 1 is black.

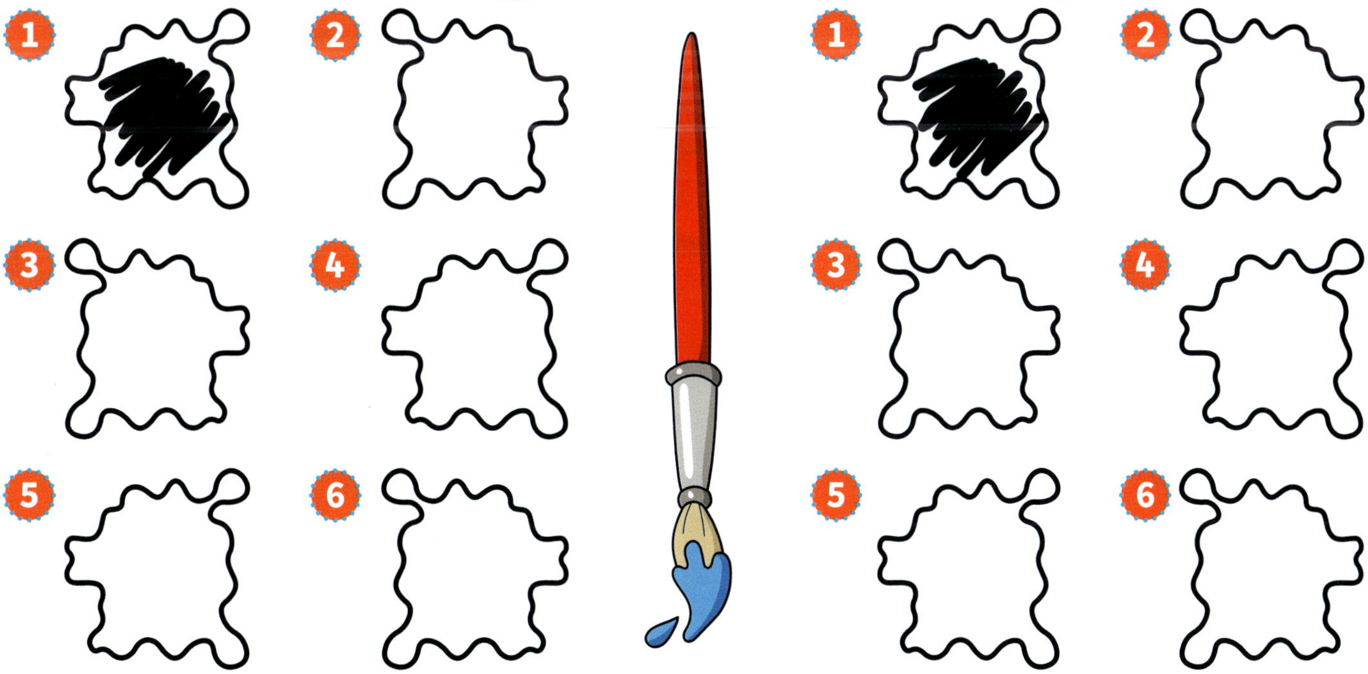

Monty's sounds

1 🎧 45 ▶ **Watch and say.**

2 **Ask and answer.**

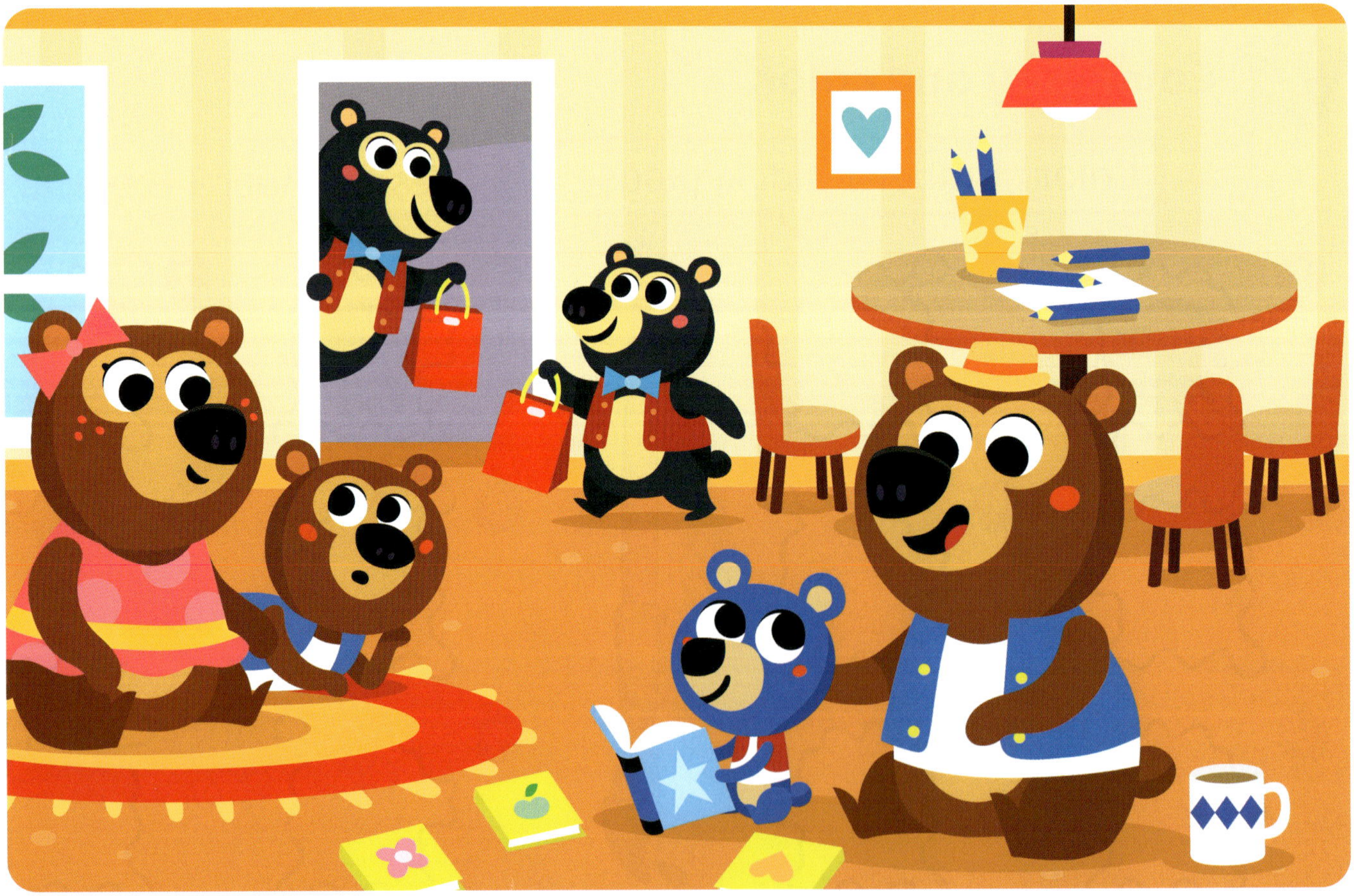

Sounds: *br*own, *b*ear, *b*lue, *b*ag, *b*lack, *b*ook

1 🎧 46 Listen and stick.

2 🎧 47 Talk to Maskman.

4 My toys

1 🎧 48–49 **Listen and point. Listen and repeat.**

2 🎵🎧 50 **Say the chant. Do the actions.**

   Vocabulary presentation: toys

1 🎧 51 Listen and color.

1

2

3

4

2 🎧 52 Listen and draw lines.

1 2 3 4

Do the online activities on **Practice Extra** as you complete this unit.

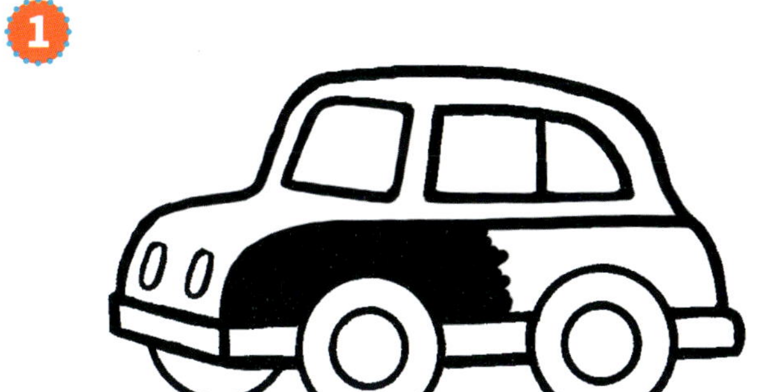

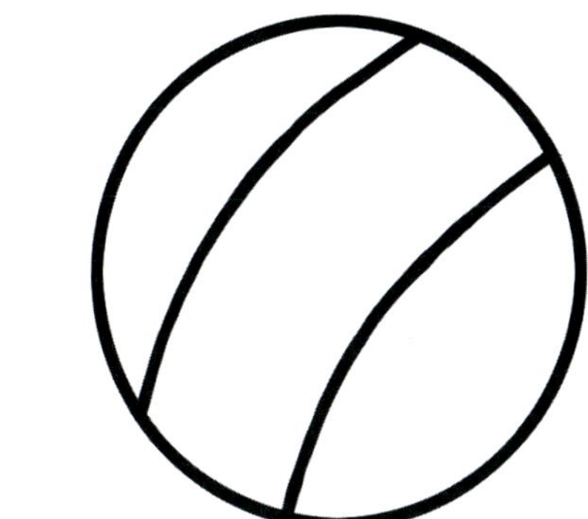

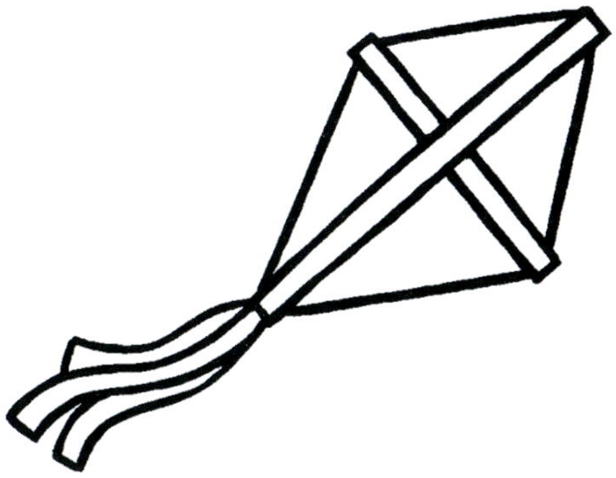

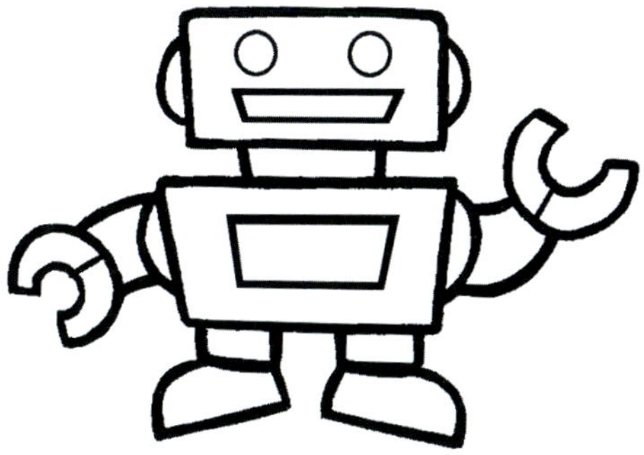

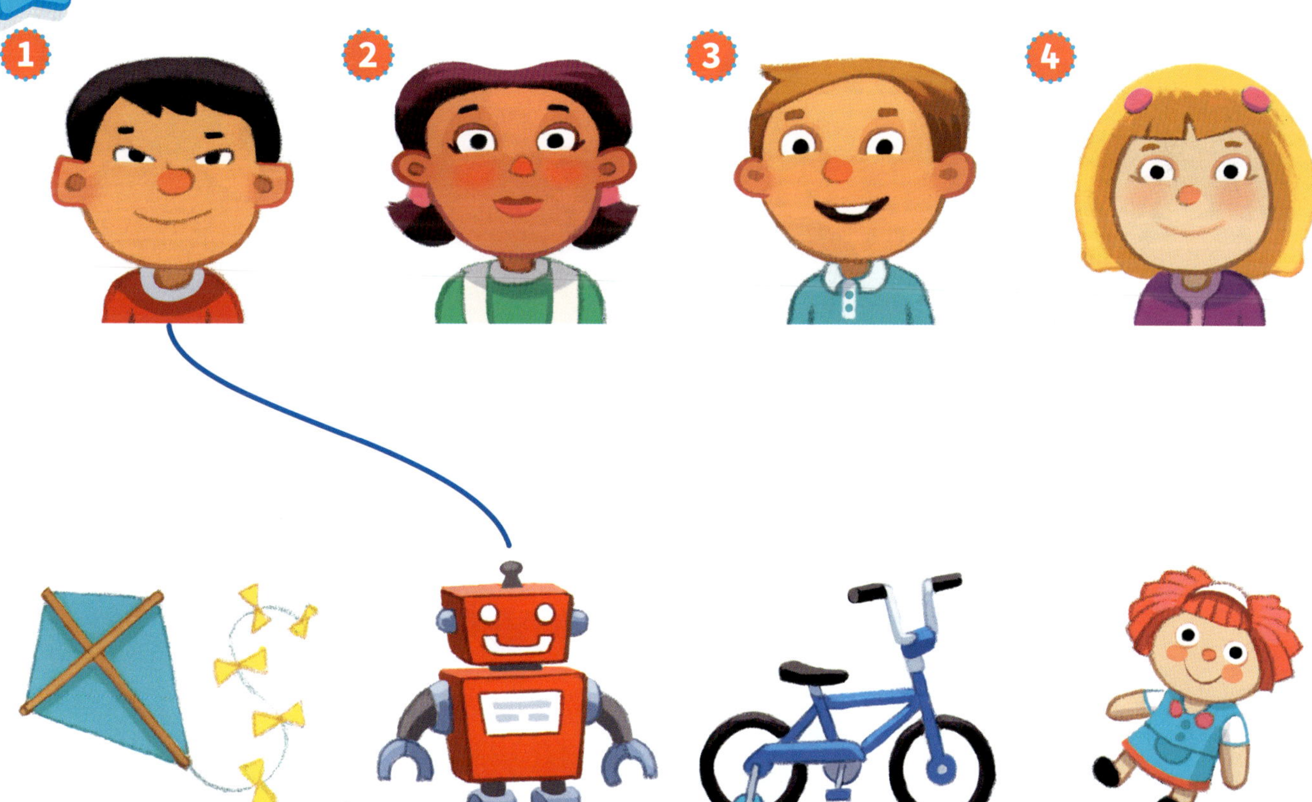

2 **Ask and answer.**

Language presentation: *Where's the car? It's here.*

1 🎧 55 ▶ Listen and write the number.

2 Draw your favorite toy. Say.

1 🎧 56 ▶ Watch the video. Listen and act out the story.

Story: unit language in context

1 🎧 57 Listen and circle. Say.

1
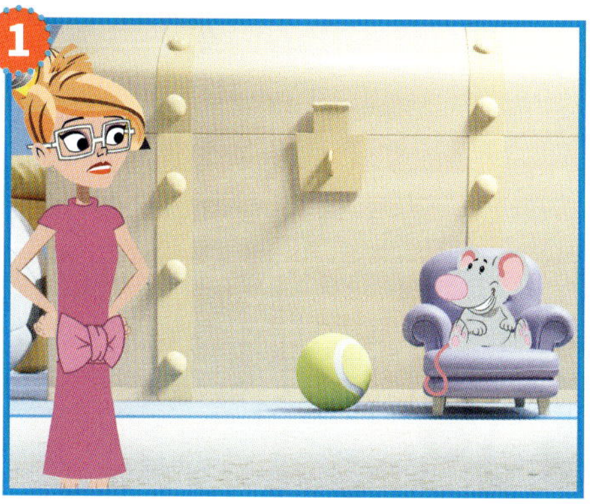
✓ ✗

2
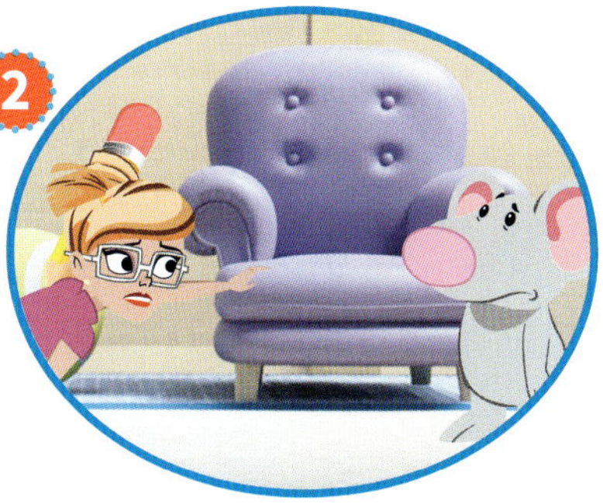
✓ ✗

3
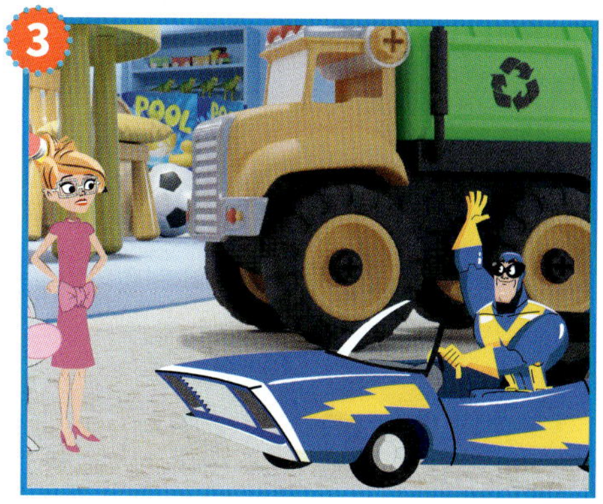

✓ ✗

4
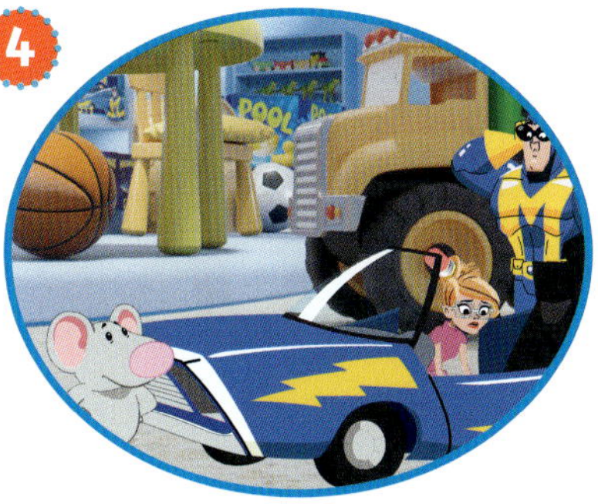

✓ ✗

5
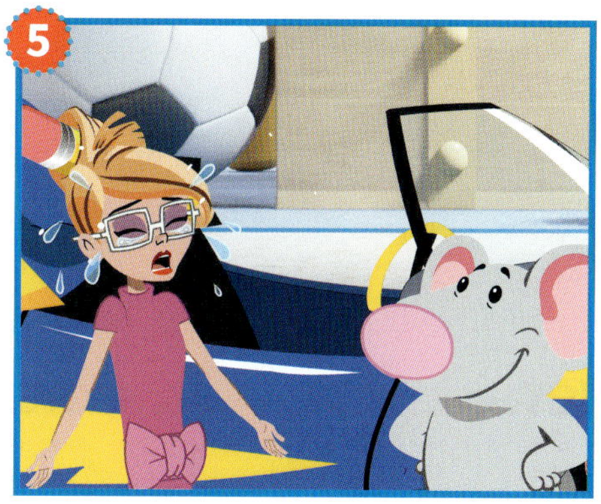
✓ ✗

6
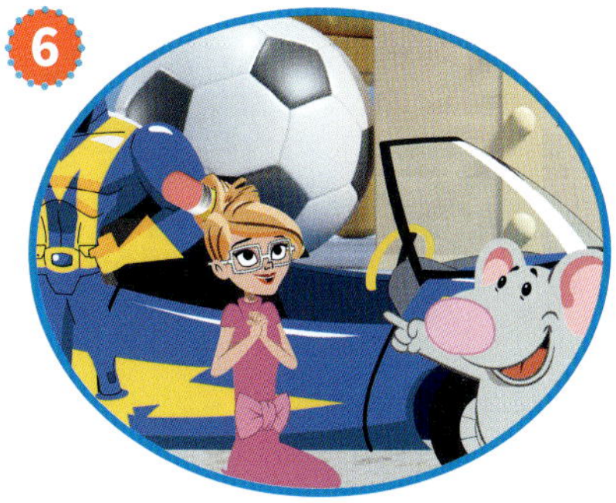
✓ ✗

2 Draw and color. Ask and answer.

What's your toy?

It's a brown doll.

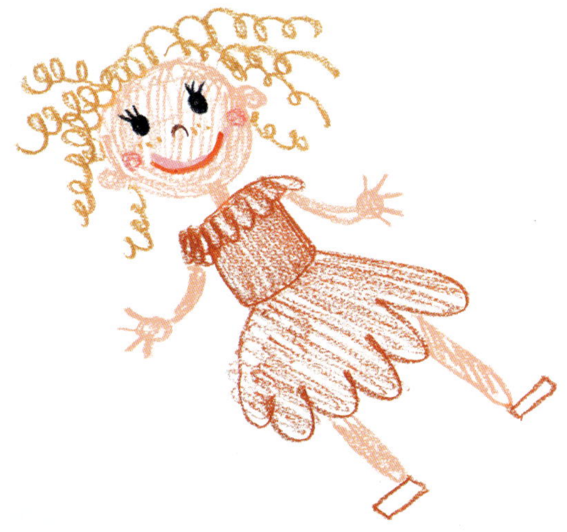

Monty's sounds

1 🎧 58 ▶ **Watch and say.**

2 **Ask and answer.**

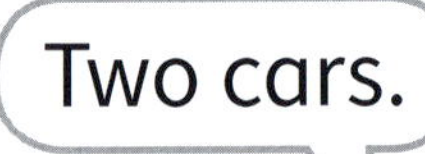

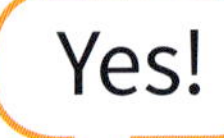

40   **Sounds:** <u>c</u>at, bla<u>ck</u>, <u>b</u>ike, <u>c</u>ow, <u>c</u>ar, <u>k</u>ite

1 🎧 59 Listen and stick.

2 🎧 60 Talk to Maskman.

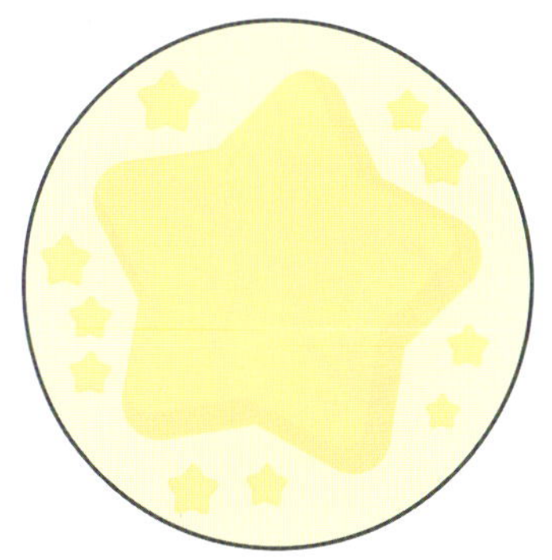

Marie's art

What is symmetry?

1 ▶ **Watch the video. Answer.**

2 🎧 61 **Listen, point, and say. Listen and color.**

3 **Look and put a ✓ or an X.**

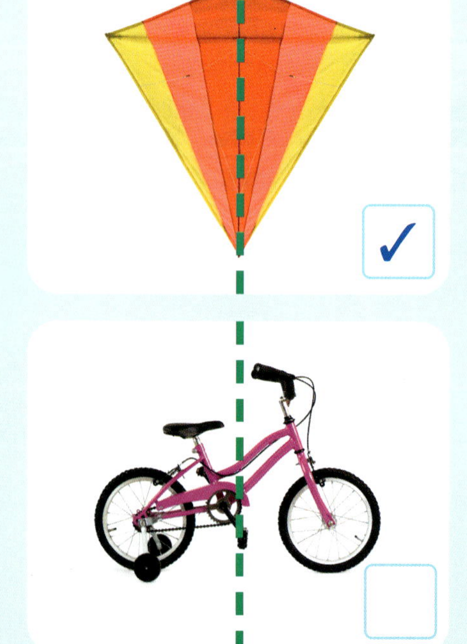 ✓

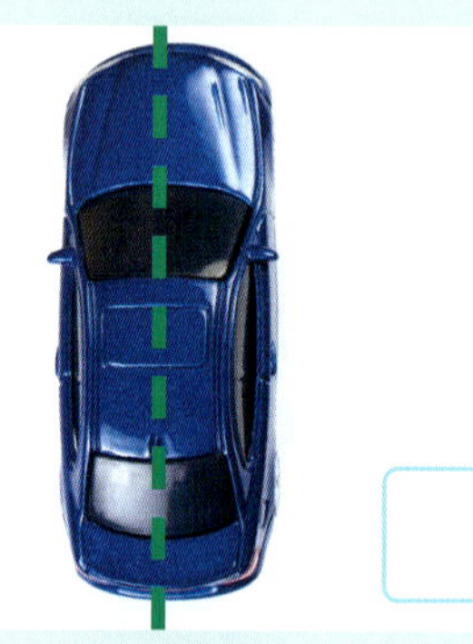

4 Look and trace. Color and say.

1

2

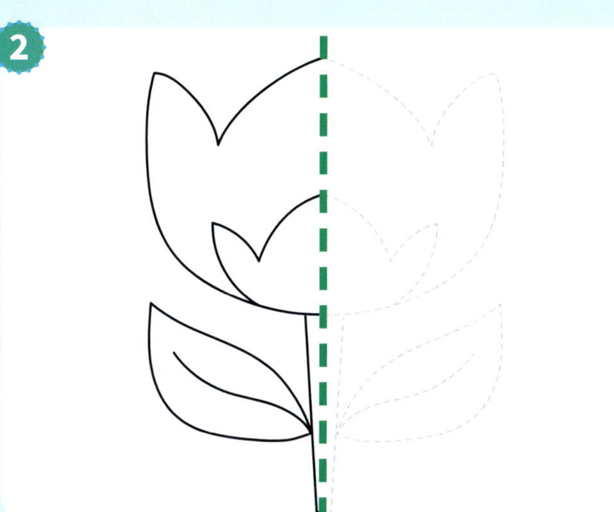

5 Look and draw. Draw for your friend.

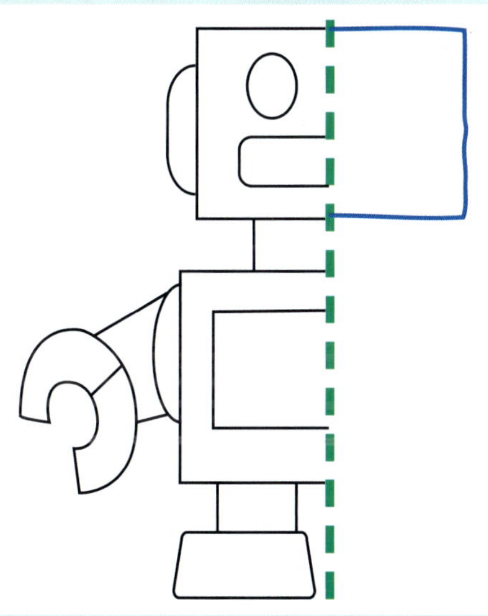

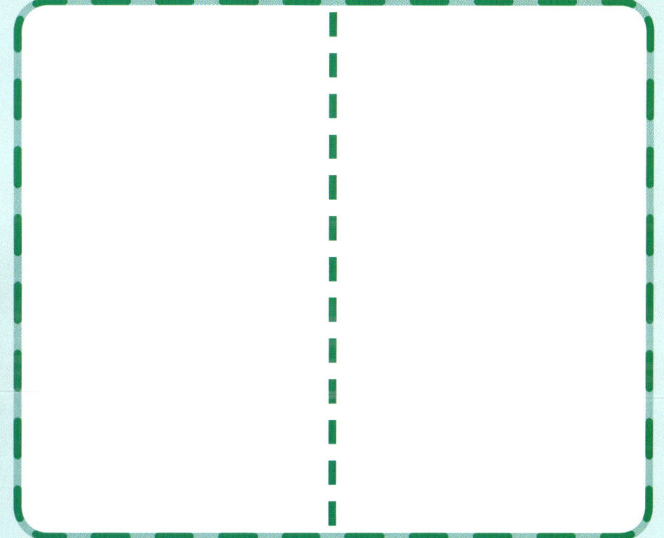

Project

Paint a symmetrical picture.

Maskman's practice

1 🎧 62 **Listen and check (✓). Act it out.**

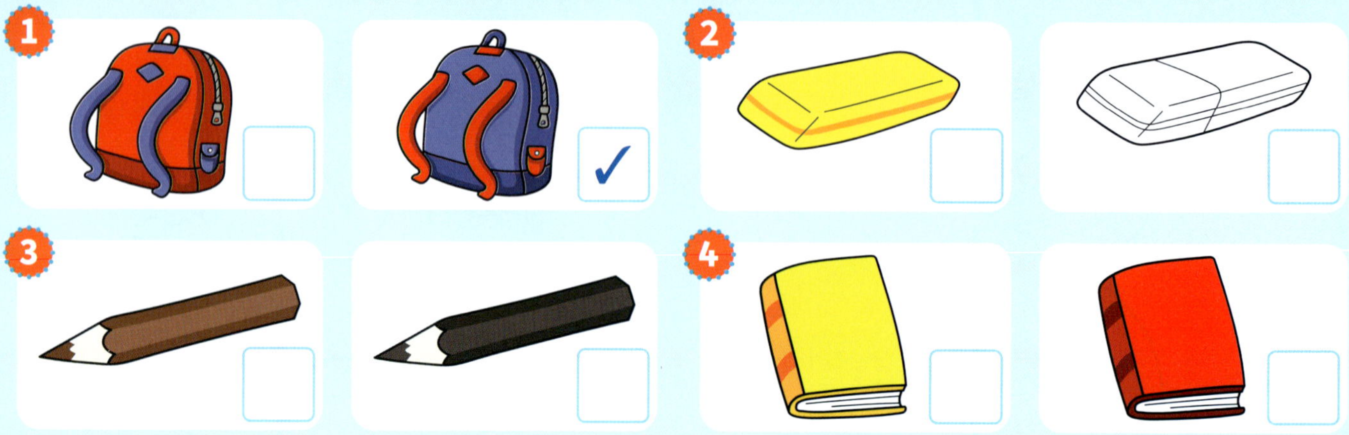

2 **Count and write the number. Say.**

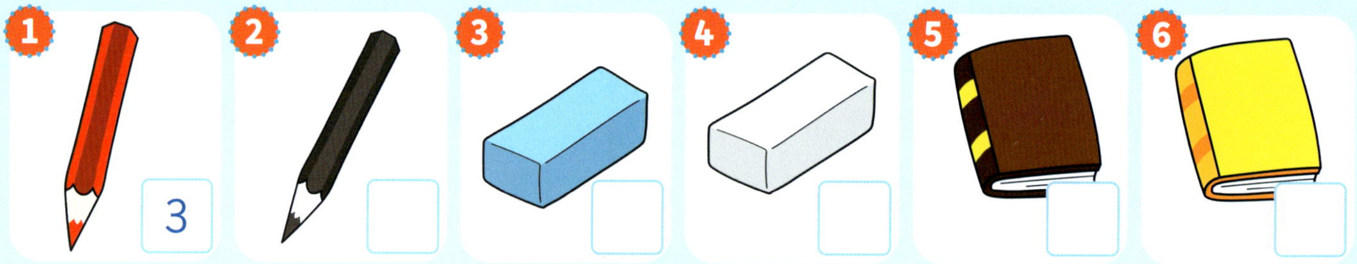

1. 3

3 **Listen and write the number.**
Listen and color.

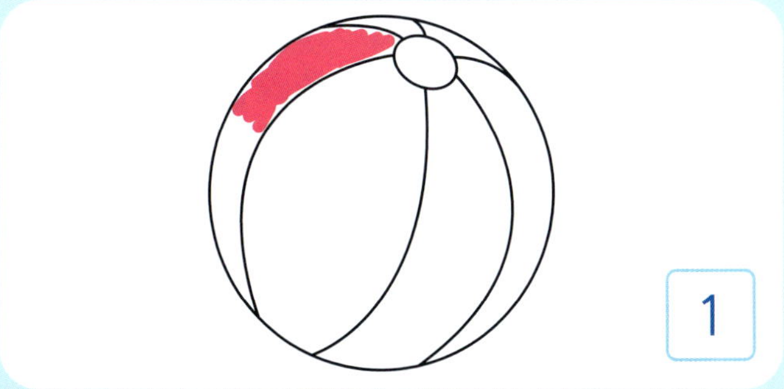

1

4 **Look and complete.**

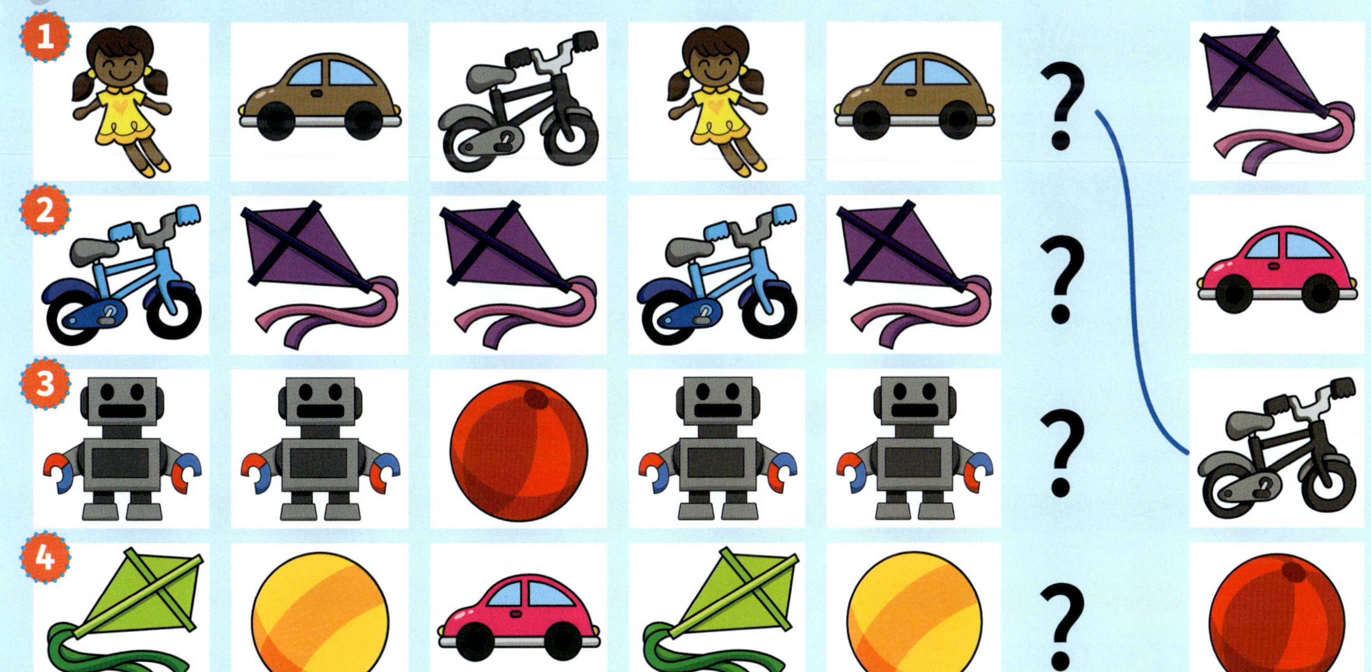

Trevor's values

Giving

 🎧 64 **Listen and point.**

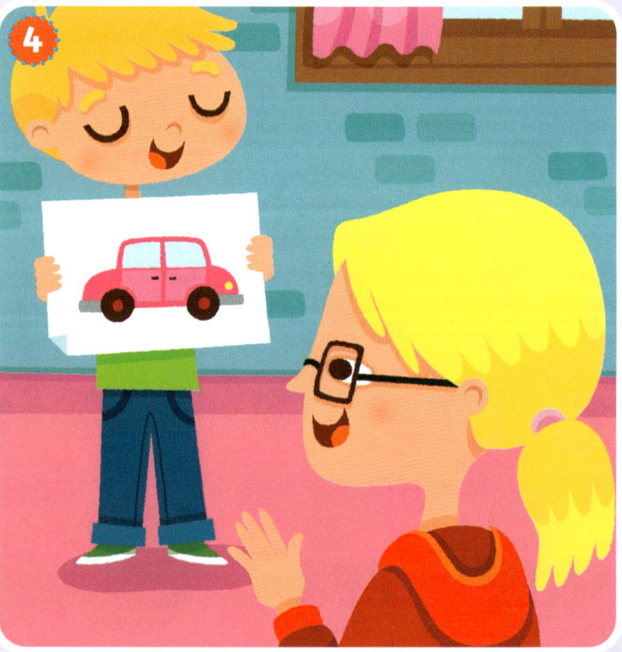

2 **Act it out.**

Giving: *Mommy, Daddy; Here's a kite for you.* | social responsibilities

1 🎧 65 Listen and color.

2 🎧 66 Listen and write the number.

1 🎧 67–68 **Listen and point. Listen and repeat.**

2 🎵🎧 69 **Say the chant. Do the actions.**

Vocabulary presentation: home

1 🎧 70 Listen and circle.

2 🎧 71 Listen and color.

1 72–73 Listen and point. Sing the song.

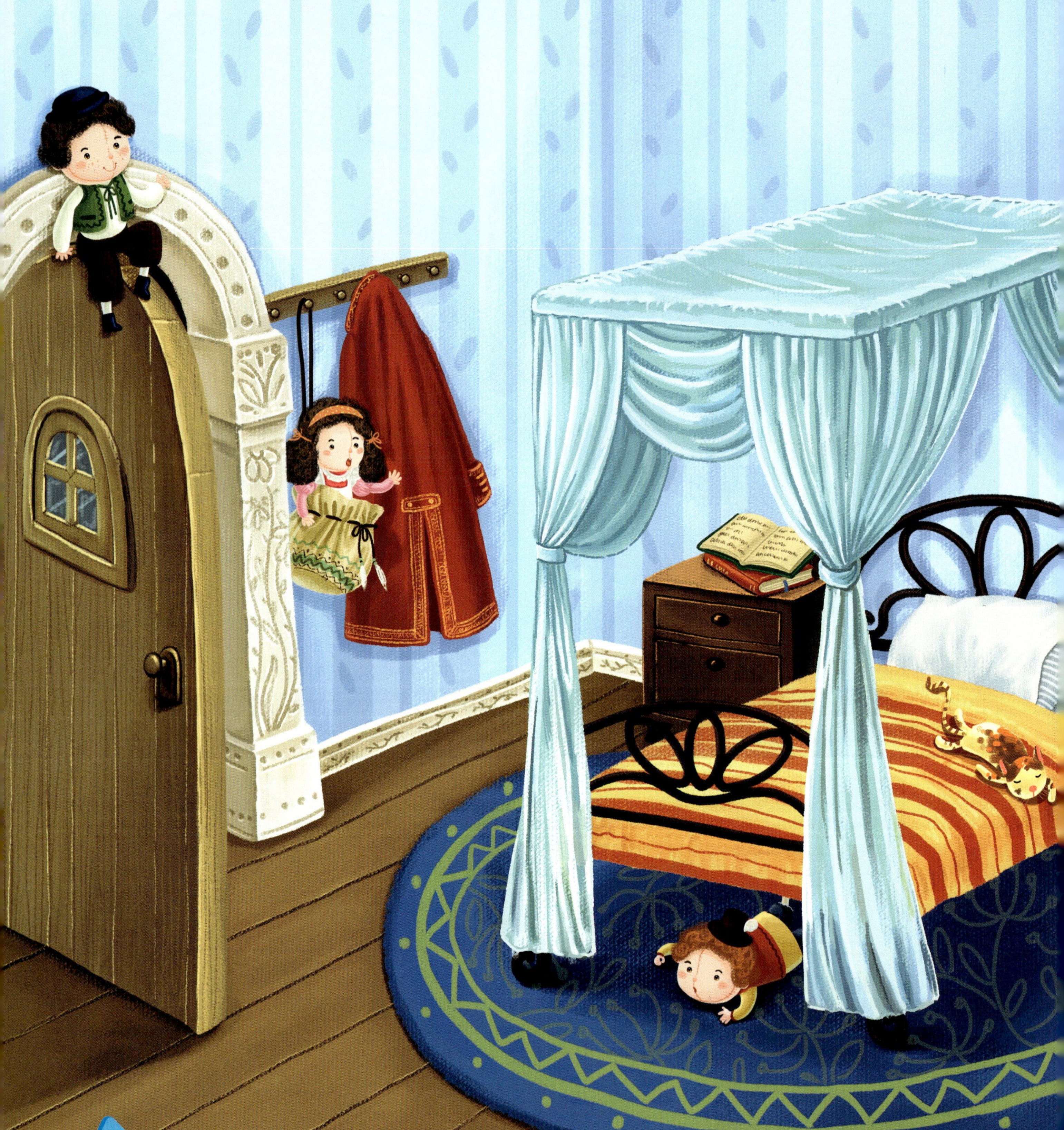

2 Say and point.

She's in the bag.

Here!

Language presentation: *She's in the bag.*

1 🎧 74 ▶ Listen and draw lines.

1
2
3
4

2 🎧 75 Listen and follow.

1 🎧 76 ▶ Watch the video. Listen and act out the story.

 Story: unit language in context

1 🎧 77 Listen and draw lines.

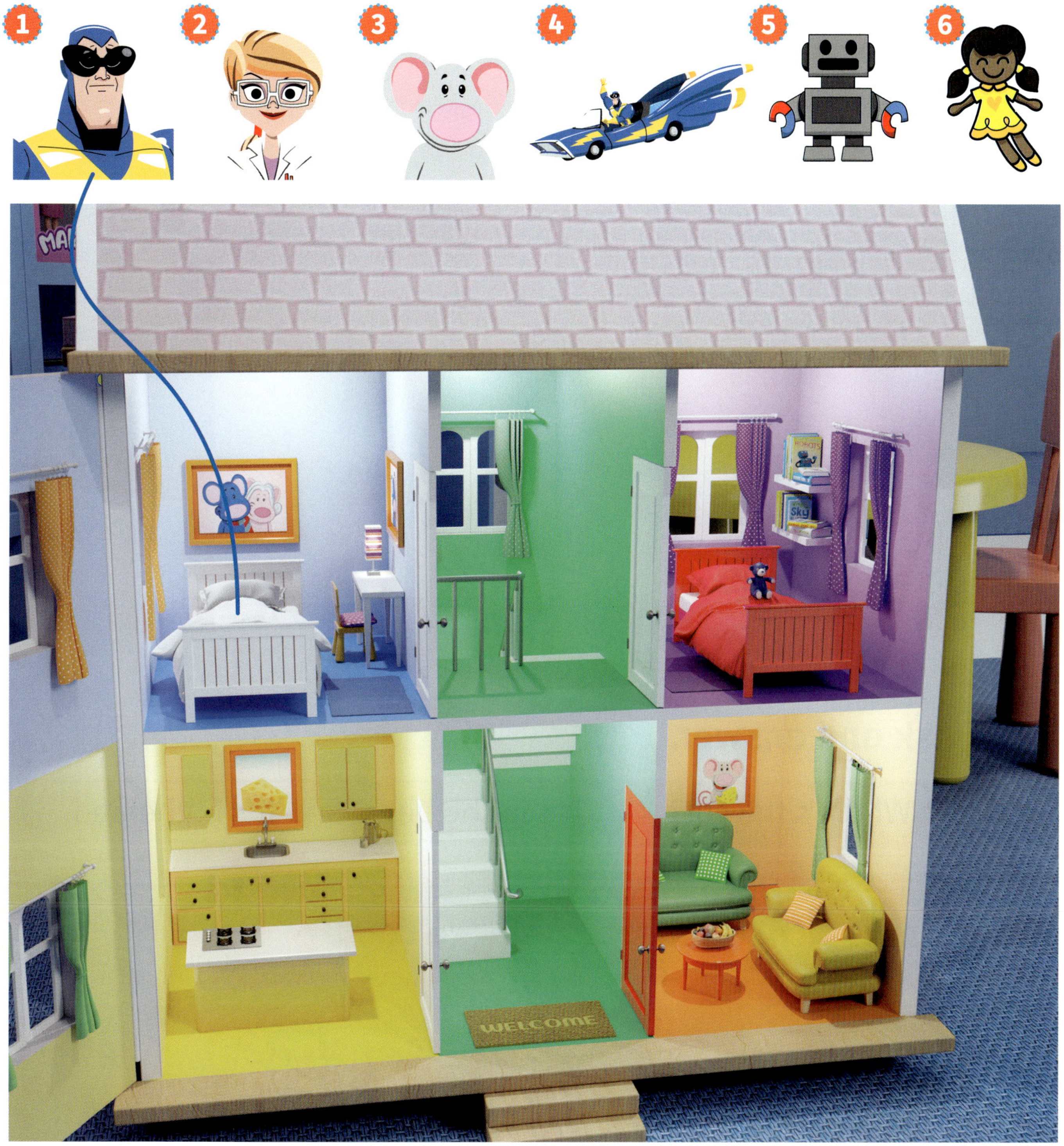

2 Ask and answer.

Monty's sounds

1 🎧 78 ▶ **Watch and say.**

2 **Ask and answer.**

Sounds: _dog_, un_d_er, _bed_, _d_uck

1 🎧 79 Listen and stick.

2 🎧 80 Talk to Maskman.

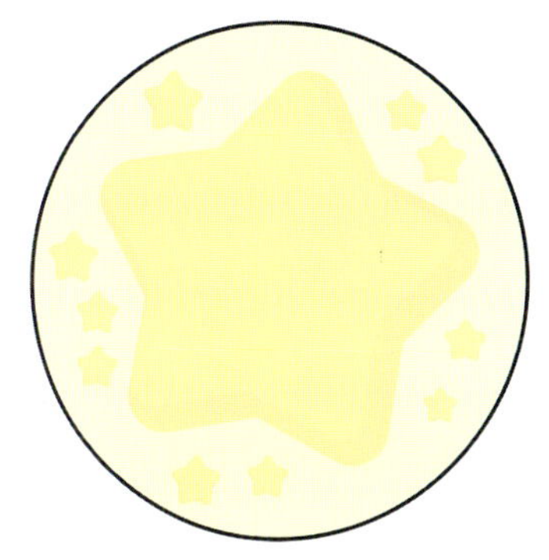

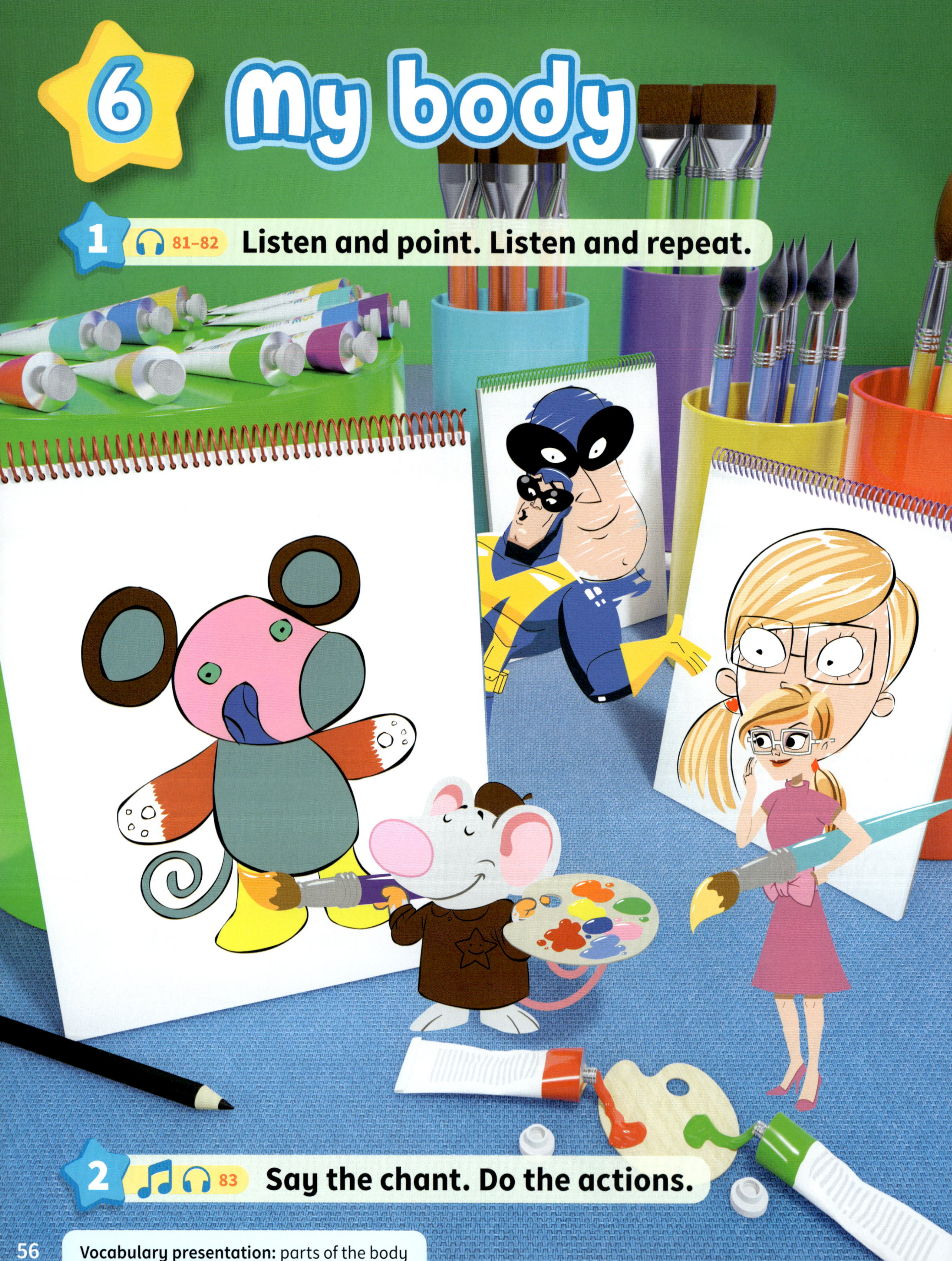

6 My body

 Vocabulary presentation: parts of the body

1 84 Listen and write the number.

1

2 Look and complete.

1
2
3
4

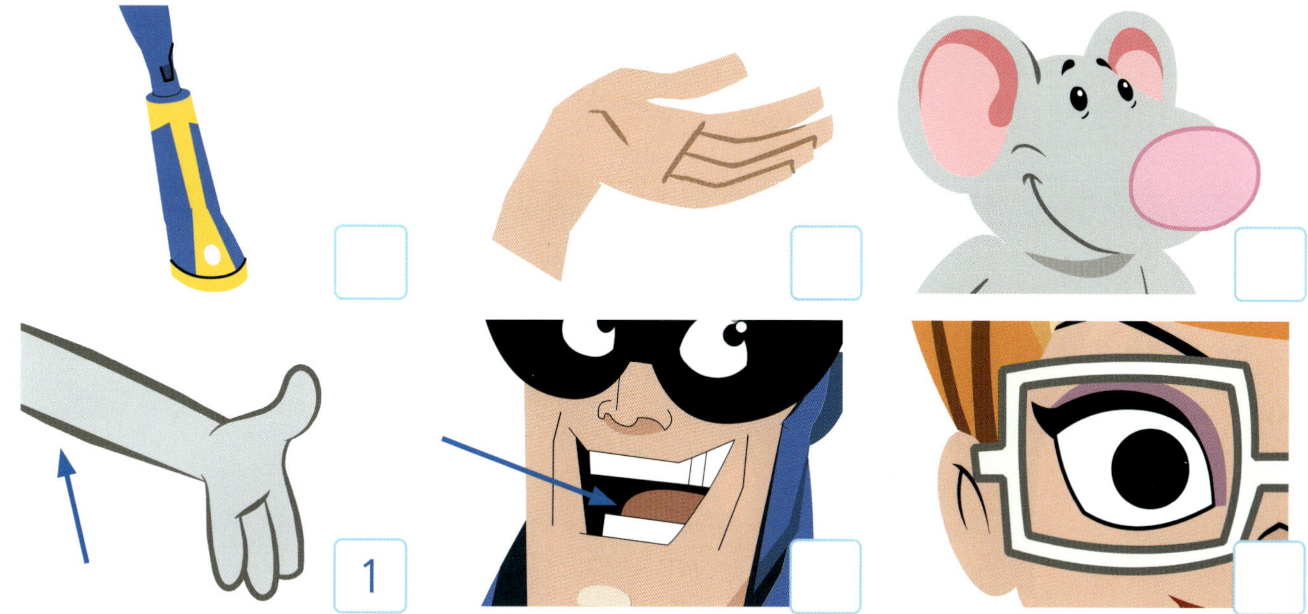

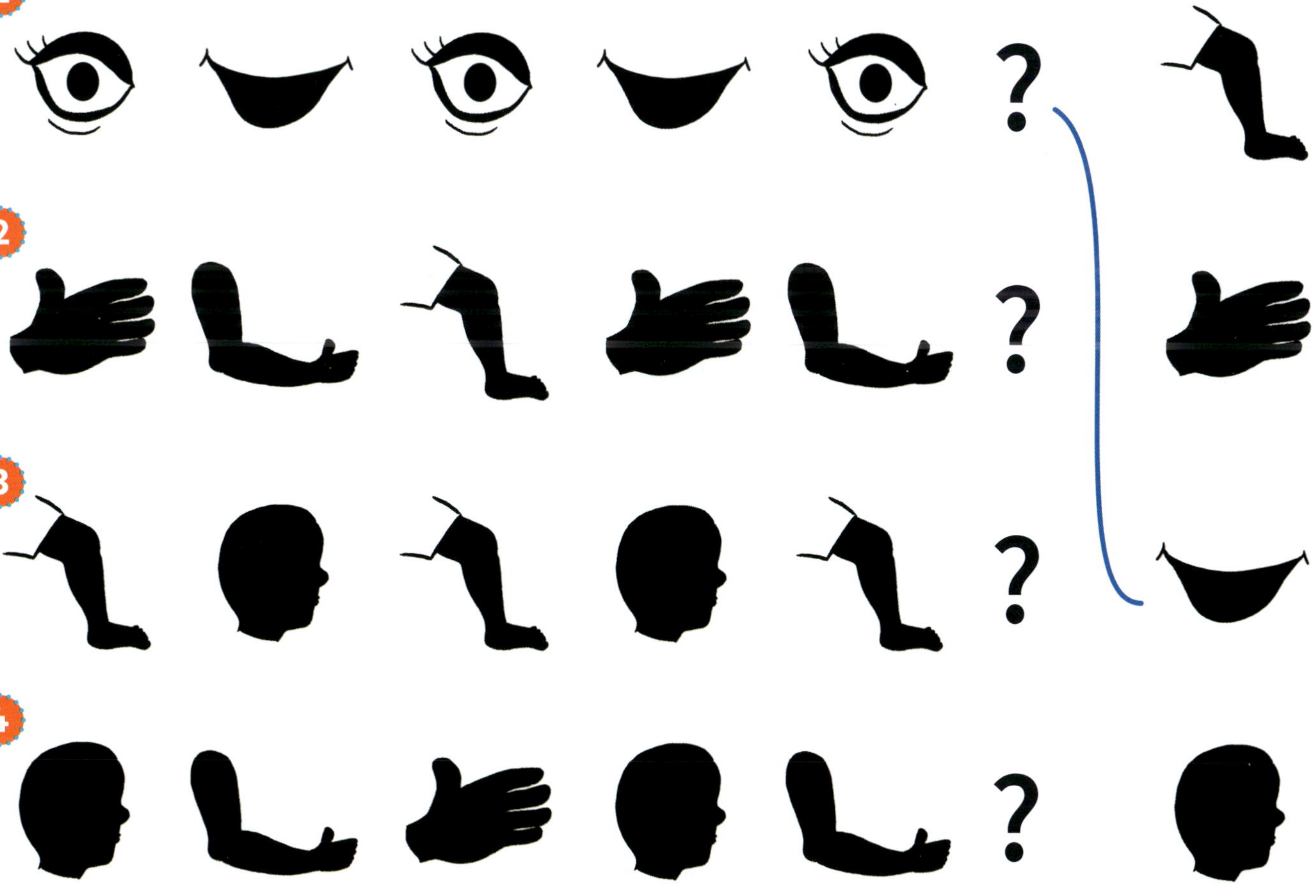

Do the online activities on Practice Extra as you complete this unit.

Language presentation: *I have four hands.*

1  Listen and check (✓).

2  Draw an alien. Say.

1 🎧 88 ▶ **Watch the video. Listen and act out the story.**

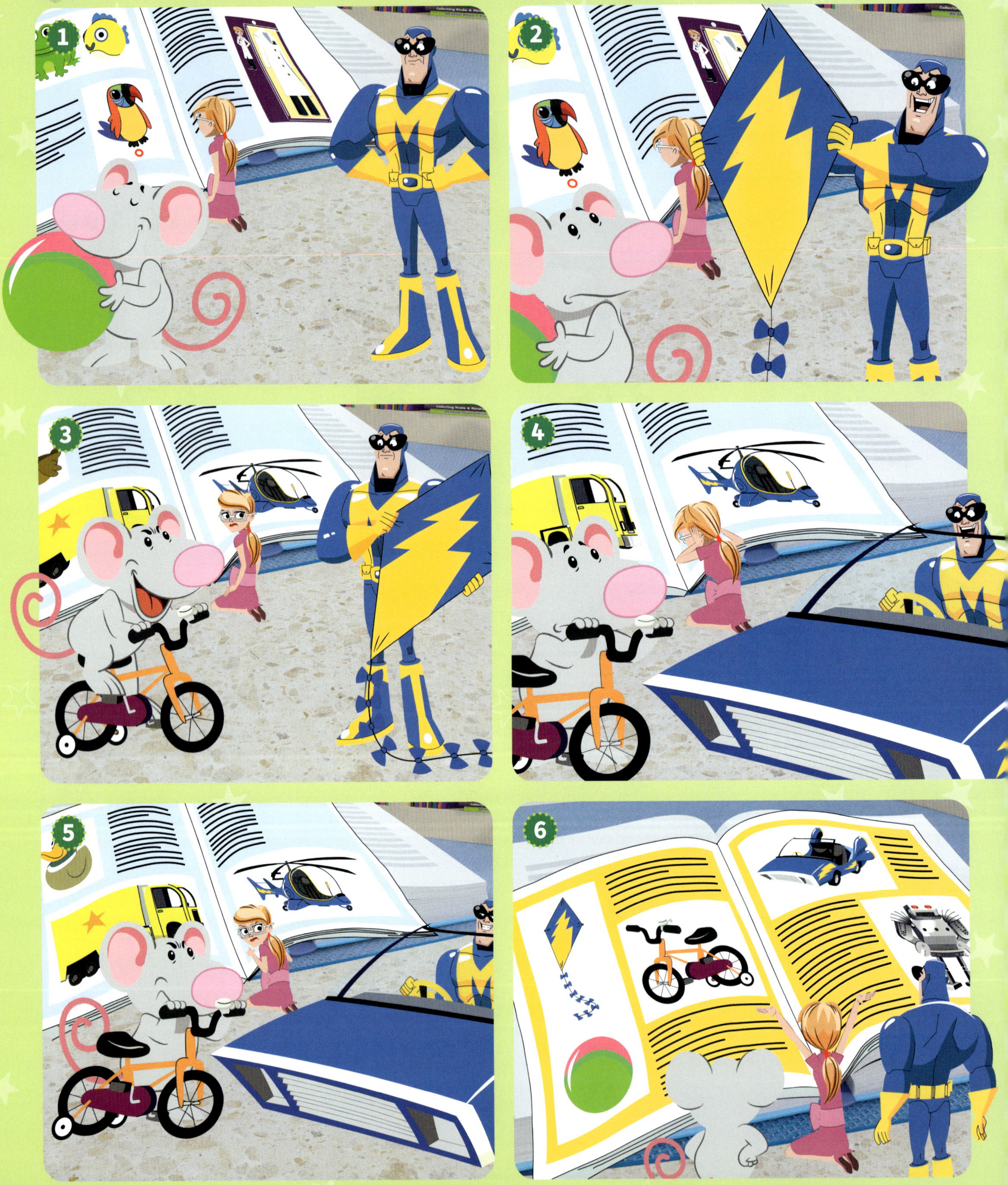

1 🎧 89 Listen and circle. Say.

1

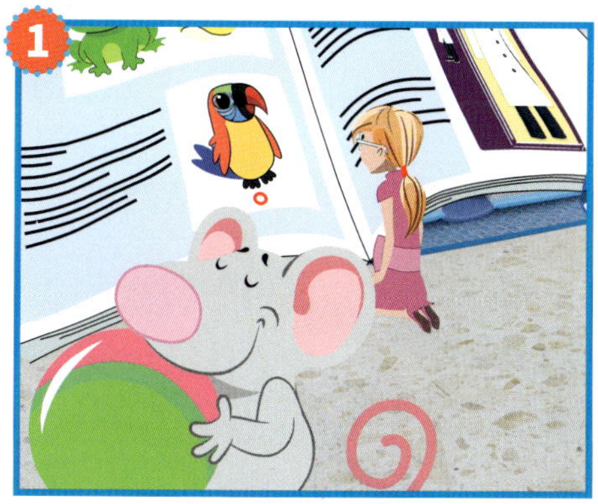

✓ ✗

2

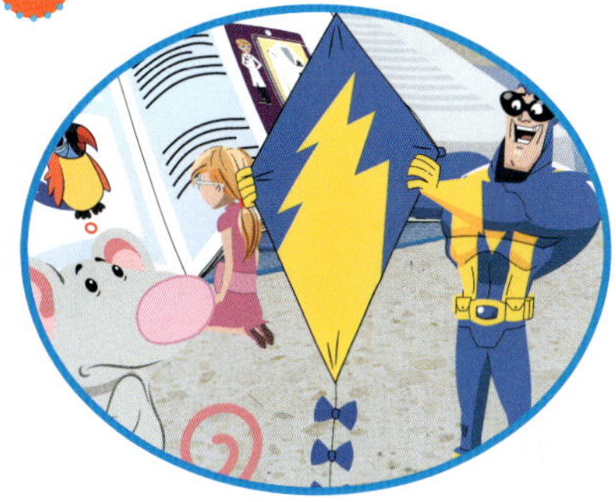

✓ ✗

3

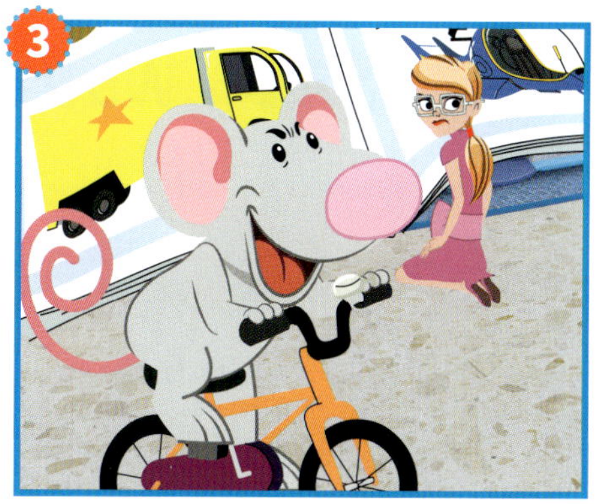

✓ ✗

4

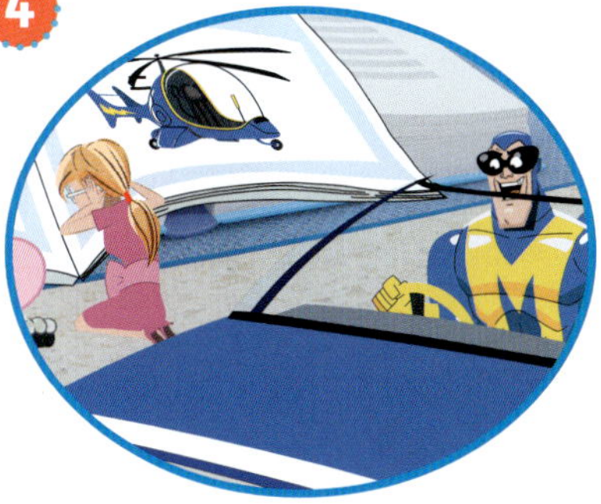

✓ ✗

5

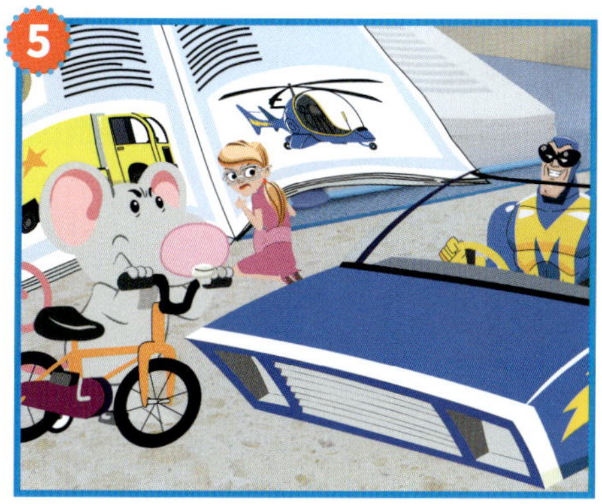

✓ ✗

6

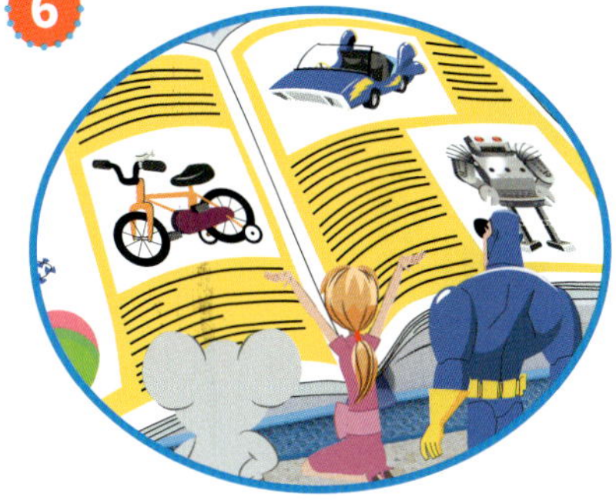

✓ ✗

2 Draw a line (→ ↘ ↗). Say.

I have five gray legs.

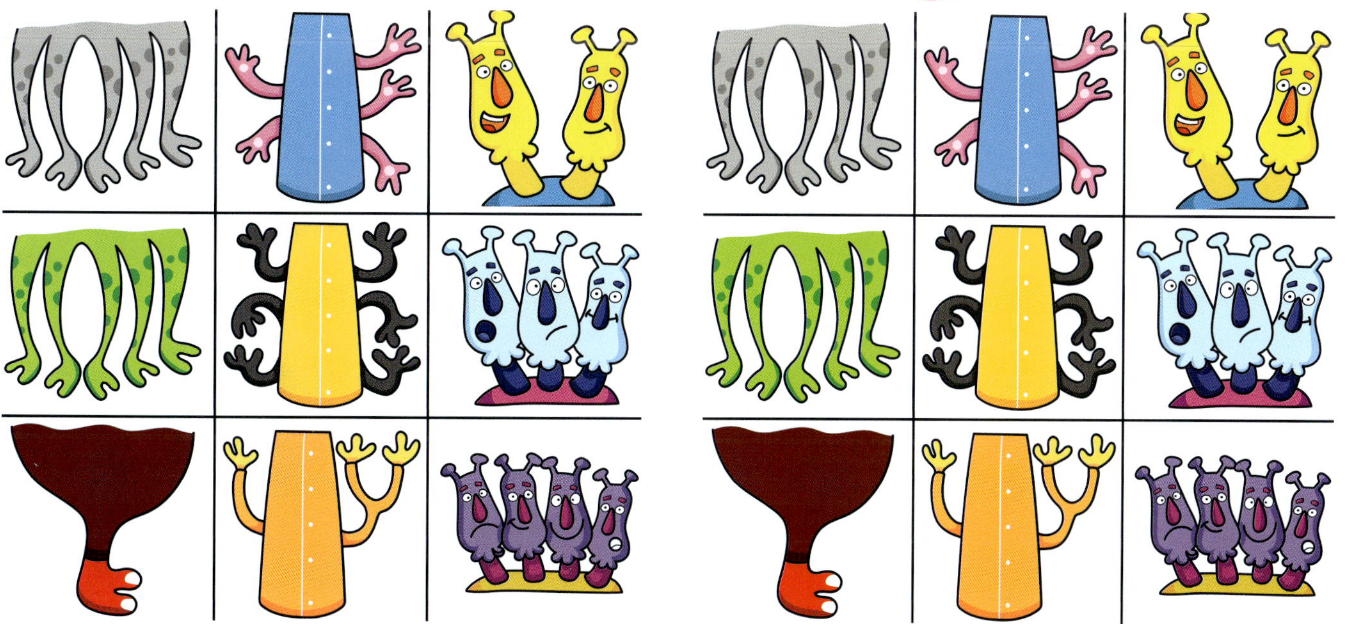

Monty's sounds

1 🎧 90 ▶ **Watch and say.**

2 **Choose, draw, and say.**

 Sounds: _egg_, _bed_, _leg_, _head_

1 🎧 91 Listen and stick.

2 🎧 92 Talk to Maskman.

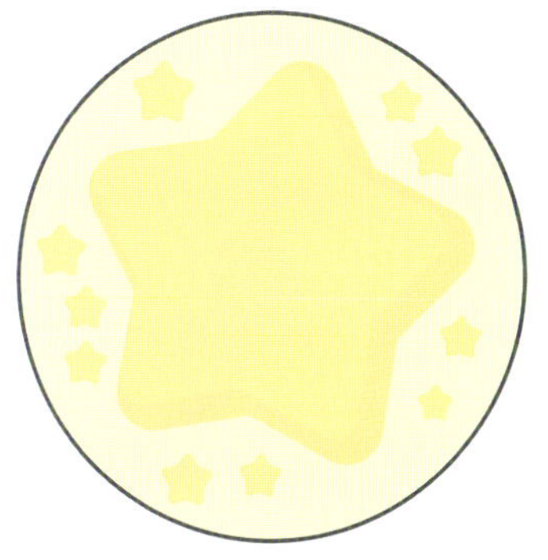

Marie's art

How can we make art?

1 ▶ **Watch the video. Answer.**

2 🎧 93 **Listen and write the number. Say.**

3 **Look and draw lines.**

4 Look and say the body part. Draw.

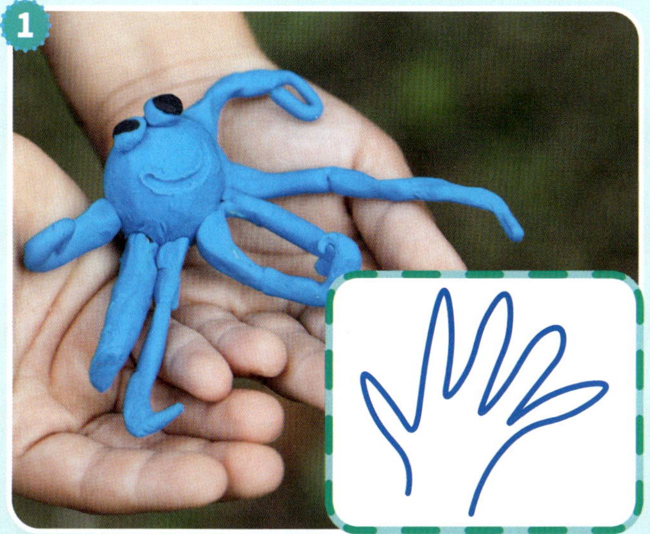

5 Talk about art you make.

Project

Use your hands to create art.

Maskman's practice

1 🎧 94 **Listen and write the number.**

2 **Draw and color. Say and color.**

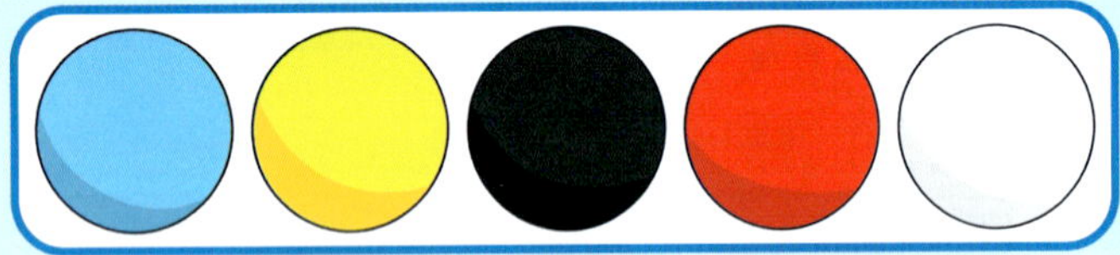

3
95
Listen and put a ✓ or an ✗.
1
2
3
4
✓
✗
4
Choose and color. Say and color.
I have red legs.

Trevor's values

Taking turns

 **1** 🎧 96 **Listen and point.**

2 **Act it out.**

 Taking turns: *Let's play pairs. OK. You start. It's my turn.* |  collaboration

Review Units 5 and 6

1 97 Listen and draw lines.

1

2

3

4

2 98 Listen and circle.

1

2

3

4

5

6

Remember to finish the online activities for these units on Practice Extra.

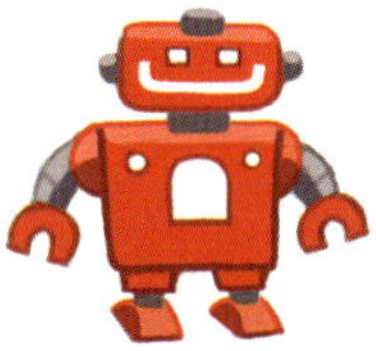

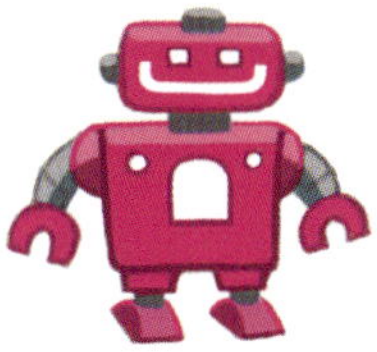

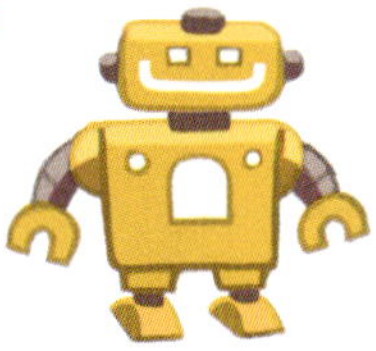

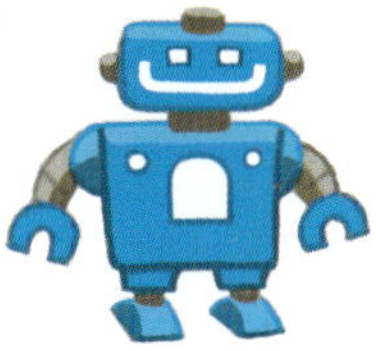

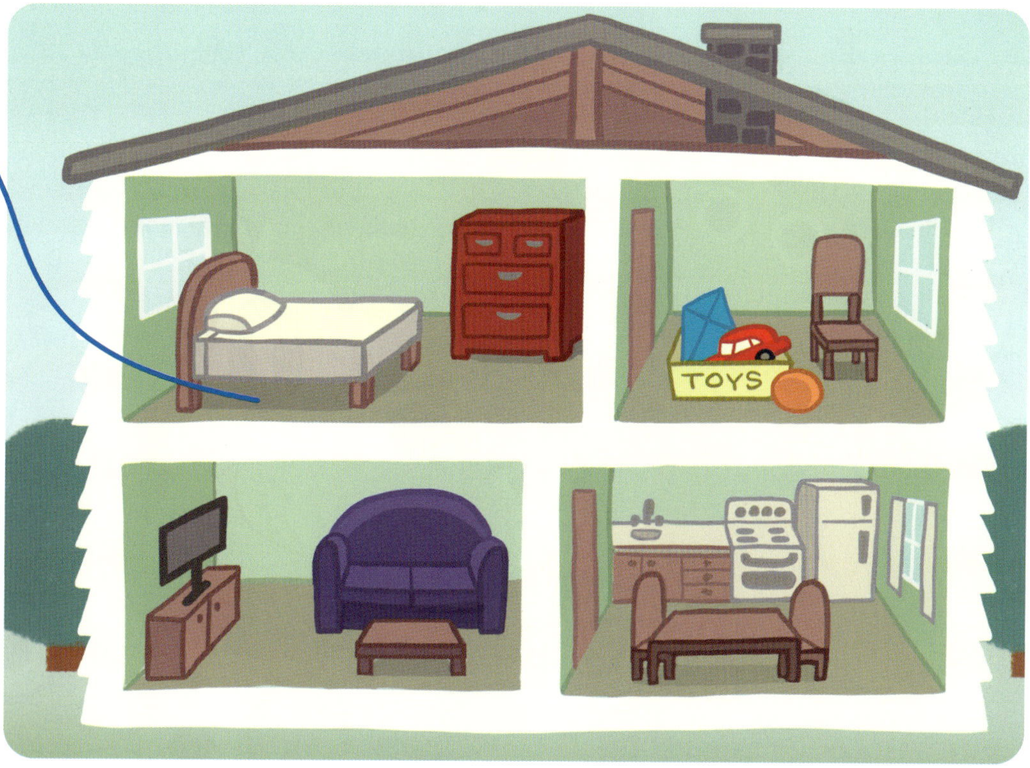

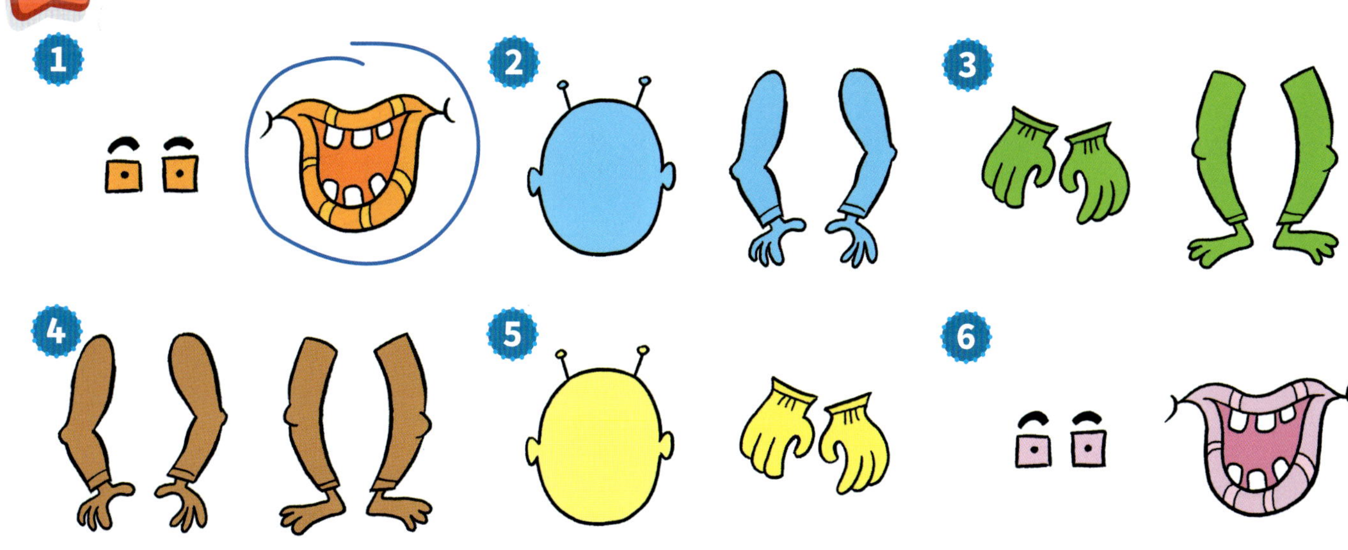

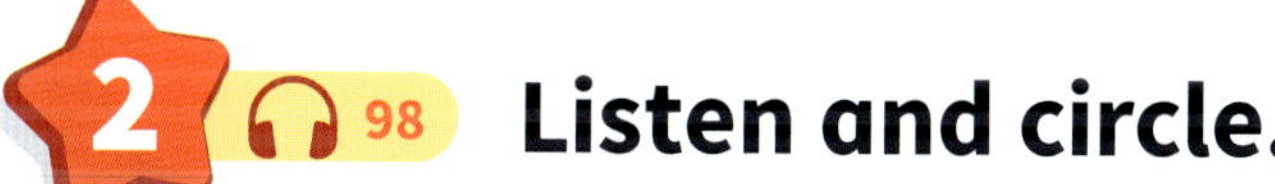

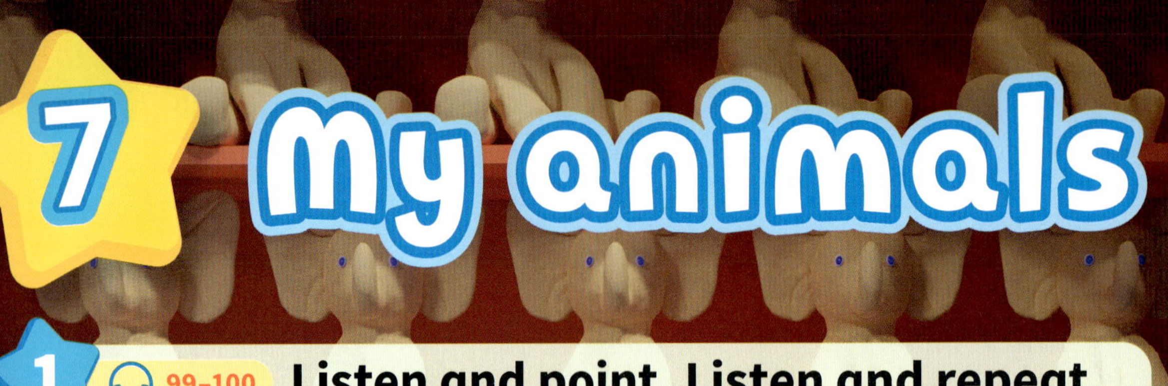

7 My animals

1 🎧 99–100 **Listen and point. Listen and repeat.**

2 🎵🎧 101 **Say the chant. Do the actions.**

Vocabulary presentation: animals

1 🎧 102 Listen and follow.

2 🎧 103 Listen and draw lines.

Language presentation: *I can jump. I can't fly.*

1 106 ▶ Listen and check (✓).

2 107 Listen and write the number.

1 🎧 108 ▶ Watch the video. Listen and act out the story.

7

1 (109) Listen and draw lines.

1 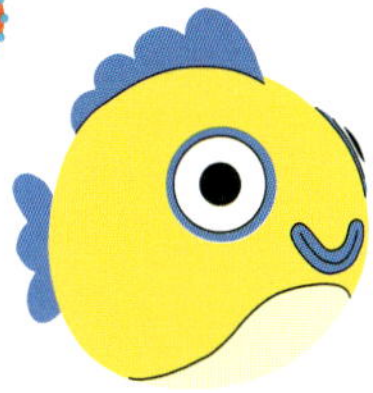

2 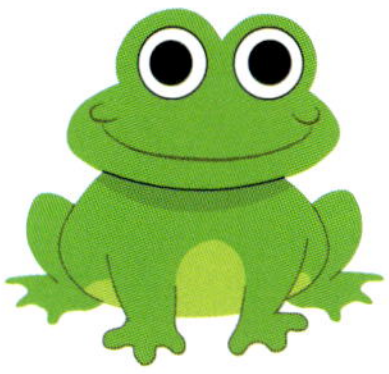

3 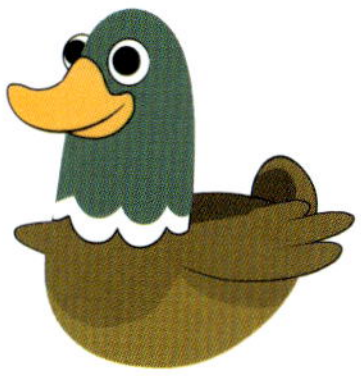

4 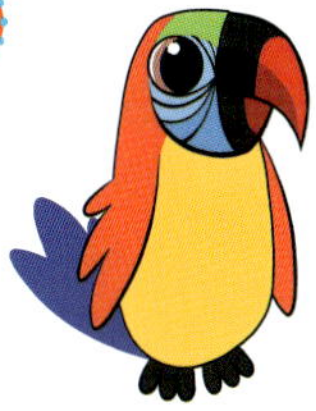

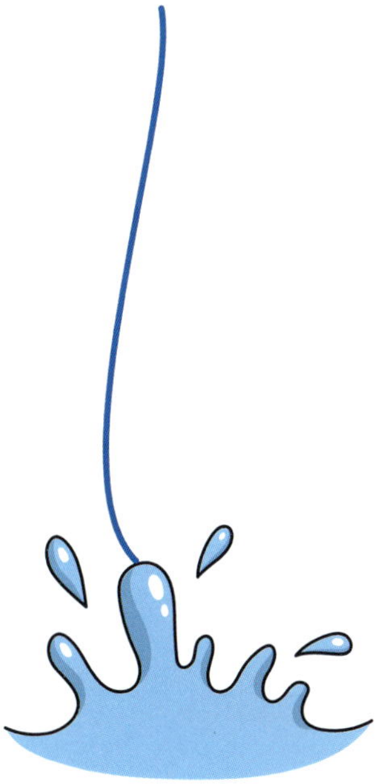

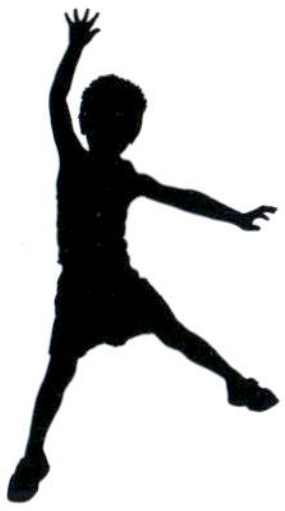

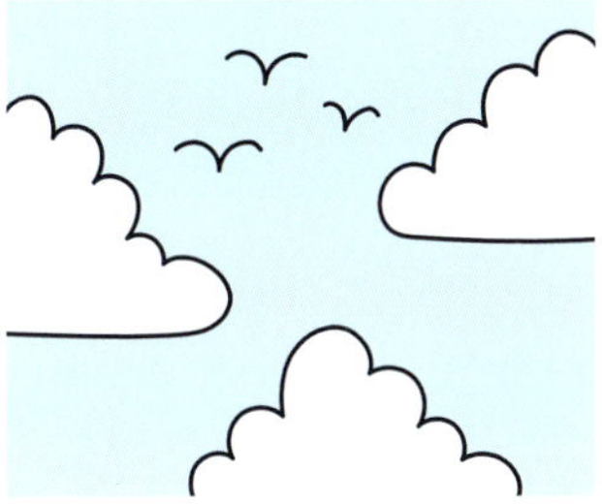

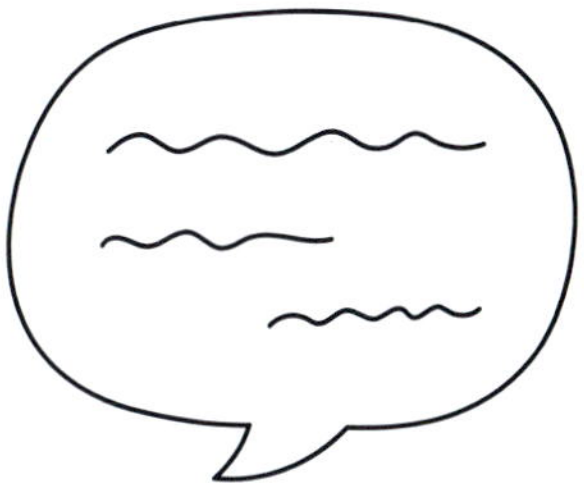

2 Put a ✓ or an ✗. Ask three friends.

Can you swim?

Yes, I can.

	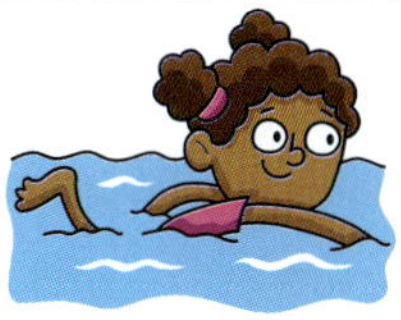	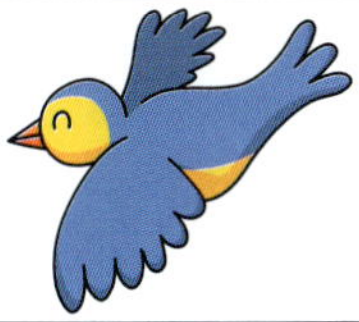	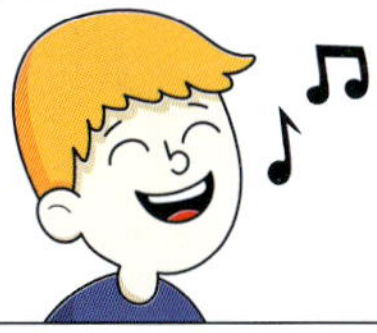	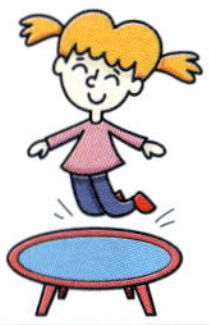
Me				
1				
2				
3				

1 🎧 110 ▶ **Watch and say.**

2 **Ask and answer.**

Sounds: _two_, _tigers_, _cat_, _toys_, _not_

1 🎧 111 Listen and stick.

2 🎧 112 Talk to Maskman.

8 My food

1 113–114 **Listen and point. Listen and repeat.**

2 115 **Say the chant. Do the actions.**

Vocabulary presentation: food

 **116**  **Listen and circle.**

 **Look and complete.**

Language presentation: *I like fruit. I don't like milk.*

 **119** ▶ **Listen and write the number.**

2 **Draw food you like and don't like. Say.**

Me! 🙂

Me! ☹

Language practice: *I like fruit. I don't like milk.*

1 🎧 120 ▶ Watch the video. Listen and act out the story.

1  121 **Listen and circle. Who says it?**

1   
2   

3   
4   

5   
6   

2 **Draw lines. Tell your friend.**

   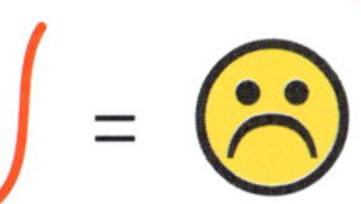

1 🎧 122 ▶ **Watch and say.**

2 **Choose and say.**

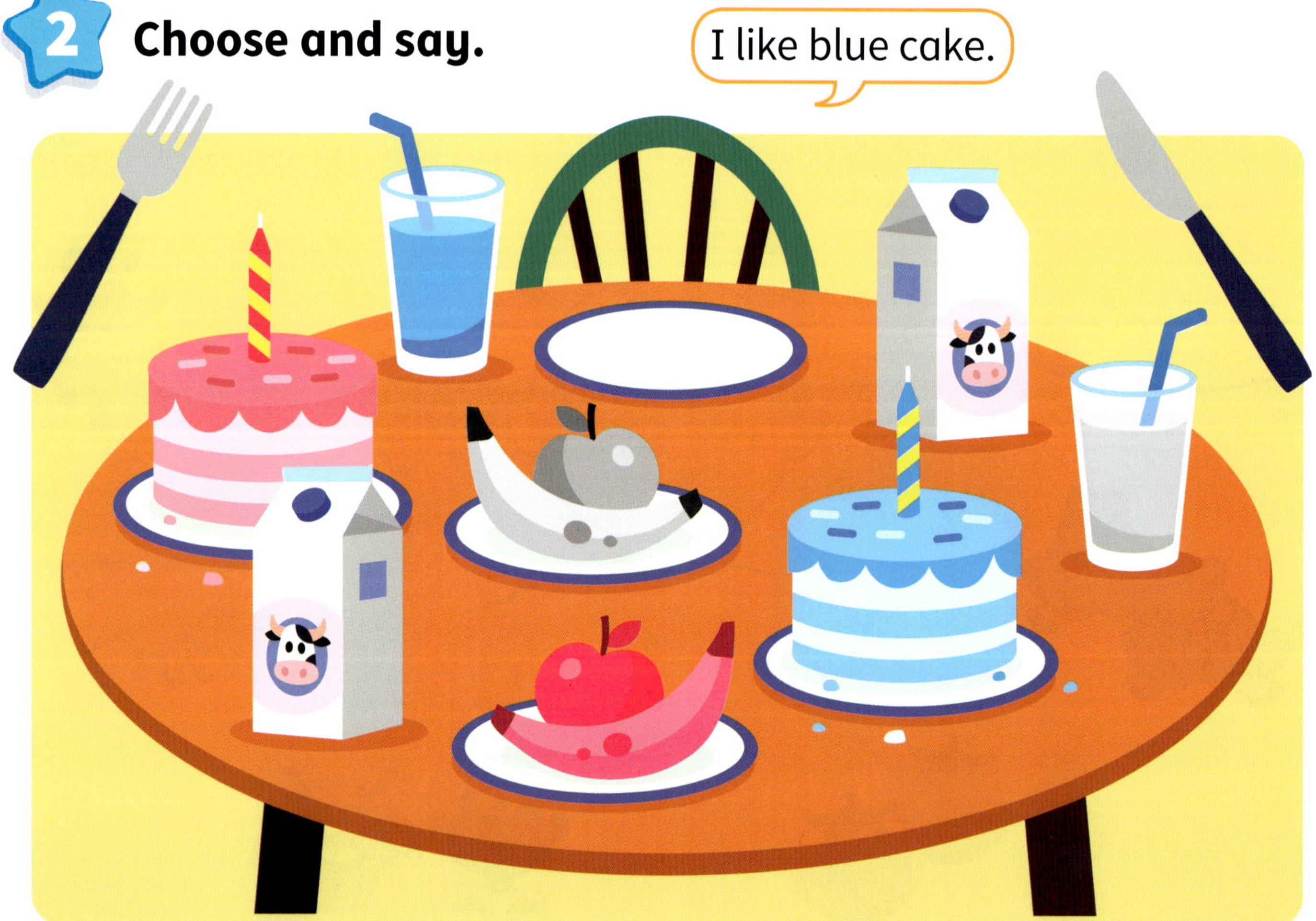

Sounds: *cake, table, gray*; *milk, pink*; *fruit, blue*

1 🎧 123 **Listen and stick.**

1	2	3
4	5	6

2 🎧 124 **Talk to Maskman.**

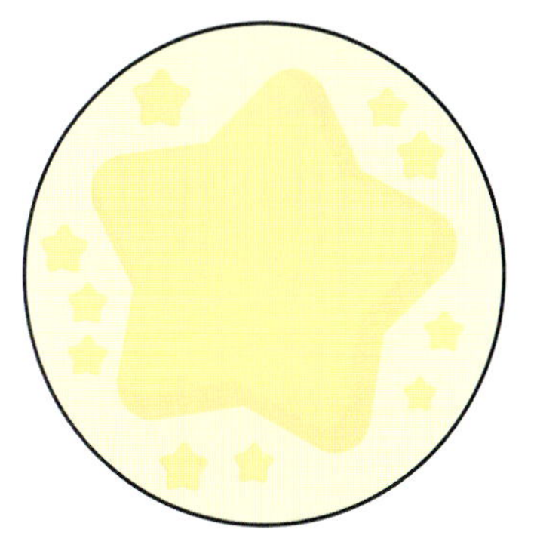

Is it sweet or savory?

1  **Watch the video. Answer.**

2 🎧 125 **Listen and point. Say the words.**

 **Look and circle.**

  Is it sweet or savory? | 🛡 critical thinking

4 🎧 126 Listen and draw lines.

 5 Talk about your favorite food.

Project

Make sweet and savory food plates.

Maskman's practice

1 **Count and write. Ask and answer.**

  4

2 **Point and say.**

3 🎧 127 Find groups of three. Draw lines. Listen and check.

4 Play and say.

Sharing

 🎧 128 **Listen and point.**

 **Act it out.**

1 🎧 129 **Listen and color.**

2 🎧 130 **Listen and draw lines.**

BATH

32
31
30
29
18
19
20
17
16
15
14
13
START
1
2
3
4

28
27
26
25
24
23
22
21
12
11
10
9
8
7
6
5

Thanks and Acknowledgments

Authors' thanks

Many thanks to everyone at Cambridge University Press & Assessment for their dedication and hard work, and in particular to:

Liane Grainger and Lynn Townsend for supervising the whole project and guiding us calmly through the storms;

Alison Bewsher for her keen editorial eye, enthusiasm, and great suggestions;

Eve Conway for great suggestions and sound editorial contribution;

We would also like to thank all our students and colleagues, past, present, and future, at Star English academy in Murcia, especially Jim Kelly for his friendship and support throughout the years.

Dedications

For my parents, Eric and Pauline, with much love and gratitude. – CN
For Shirley and Neville, love – MT

The authors and publishers acknowledge the following sources of copyright material and are grateful for the permissions granted. While every effort has been made, it has not always been possible to identify the sources of all the material used, or to trace all copyright holders. If any omissions are brought to our notice, we will be happy to include the appropriate acknowledgments on reprinting and in the next update to the digital edition, as applicable.

Key: U = Unit

Photography

The following photos are sourced from Getty Images.

U1: Sturti/E+; Anna Erastova/iStock/Getty Images Plus; **U2:** Marcy Maloy/DigitalVision; George Doyle/Stockbyte; Diana Duzbayeva/ Design Pics; Anna Erastova/iStock/Getty Images Plus; **U3:** Anna Erastova/iStock/Getty Images Plus; **U4:** ElementalImaging/E+; gwflash/iStock/Getty Images Plus; Kwanchai Lerttanapunyaporn/ EyeEm; carlosalvarez/E+; JoKMedia/E+; Anna Erastova/iStock/ Getty Images Plus; **U5:** Anna Erastova/iStock/Getty Images Plus; **U6:** JGI/Jamie Grill; Blend Images - Take A Pix Media; studyoritim/ E+; KidStock/Photodisc; Charles Thatcher/The Image Bank/Getty Images Plus; Mrs_2015/RooM; Anna Erastova/iStock/Getty Images Plus; U7: Anna Erastova/iStock/Getty Images Plus; U8: Tetra Images - Jamie Grill/Brand X Pictures; Westend61; Kiana Rosalez/EyeEm; fotosr/iStock/Getty Images Plus; jayk7/Moment; asikkk/iStock/ Getty Images Plus; Anna Erastova/iStock/Getty Images Plus.

The following photos are sourced from other libraries.

U2: Oleg Beloborodov/Alamy Stock Photo; **U4:** RTimages/ Alamy Stock Photo; **U6:** SpeedKingz/Shutterstock; **U8:** Silatip/ Shutterstock.

Commissioned photography: Artwork by Jen Naalchigar (Bright Agency) and photography Chris Warren of CWA Studios.

Illustrations

Blooberry (source Pronk); Copy cat; Beatrice Costamagna, c/o Pickled ink; Chris Jones; Helen Naylor, c/o Plum Pudding; Kelly Kennedy, c/o Sylvie Poggio; Melanie Sharp, c/o Sylvie Poggio; Richard Hoit, Beehive; Xian Xio, c/o Illustrationweb; Pronk media Inc; Chris Jones; Jake Mcdonald; Marek Jagucki; Matthew Scott.

Cover illustrations by Pronk Media Inc.

Video

Video acknowledgements are in the Teacher Resources on Cambridge One.

Audio

Audio managed by Hyphen Publishing, produced by New York Audio Productions and John Marshall Media

Songs composed by Robert Lee

Design and typeset

Blooberry Design.

Additional authors

Katy Kelly: Monty's Sounds

Rebecca Legros: Marie's math, art, and science

Freelance editor

Stephanie Howard

1 Hi! (page 11)
1
2
3
4
5
6
2 My class (page 19)

 My colors (page 33)

 My toys (page 41)

Talk to Maskman

5 My house
(page 55)

6 My body
(page 63)

7 My animals (page 77)

8 My food (page 85)

Talk to Maskman